The Professor's Quarters

Editors:
Alice D'Alessio
Albert DeGenova
Jude Genereaux
Susan O'Leary

After Hours Press
Oak Park, Illinois
2014

Table of Contents

About the artist
    Marie "Lucha" Skrobot 6
Foreword
    Albert DeGenova 7
Introduction
    Susan O'Leary 9
"Cleared-Away" Space
    Julie Eger 13
Jensen's Great Poem
    Albert DeGenova 17
Legacy
    Carol Doty 20
Fertile Ground
    Sue Wentz 23
The Writing Life
    Kristen Thacher 25
Mr. Blei
    Susan O'Leary 29
Writing at The Clearing with Norb Blei
    Maja Jurisic and Don Fraker 33
Jens' Dream Fulfilled
    Alice D'Alessio 36
I Am Here
    Ralph Murre 40
Clearing the Way
    Jude Genereaux 43
The Hawk in My Heart
    Sharon Auberle 47
Meeting Myself at The Clearing
    Jackie Langetieg 51
"Writing is a long journey toward an authentic self and setting"
    Candace Henneken 54
The Teacher
    Cheryl Welch 56
Finding The Way Home
    Jeannie Adwani 58
Clarity & Calm
    Catherine Hovis 60
The Perfect Gardener
    DyAnne Korda 65

Beyond Postcards
    Scott Stowell 67
Real Writers
    Laurie Kahn 70
Transformation
    Nancy Rafal 72
Coming Home to The Clearing
    Paula Kosin 74
Edith Nash, The Clearing, and Norb Blei
    Gloria Zager 77
The Year Was 1973...
    Elizabeth Pochran 80
Epilogue: "Find me in my books..."
    Jude Genereaux 83

Books by Norbert Blei 85

Patrons of *The Professor's Quarters* 86

Individual essays and artwork published herein are also protected by separate copyright which is retained by the author/artist. Copyrighted material is used here by special arrangement with the permission of the copyright holder.

The Professor's Quarters
ISBN 978-0-692-02748-6
Copyright © 2014 After Hours Press
www.afterhourspress.com

About the artist

All artwork included in this book is reproduced from original watercolor paintings by **Marie "Lucha" Skrobot.**

I first met Norb Blei in 1995 when I was a member of the staff at The Clearing. He was teaching his annual writing class and asked if I would bring him a pot of coffee mid-morning while he worked in his room in the professor's quarters. I did so each day the rest of that week and for years to come.

As we became friends, he discovered I liked to paint and encouraged me. Sometime around 2005, I gave him the watercolor of the "Professor's Quarters," which he hung in the Coop.
(ed. Norbert's converted chicken coop which he used as his work space.)

In the spring of 2011, Norb commissioned me to do a painting of the interior of the Coop along with a series of paintings in and around the Clearing grounds for a book that he envisioned. He told me he was going to use the painting I'd given him of the Professor's Quarters for the cover. That summer, I painted the collection of paintings for him, but when Norb became ill, the future of the book seemed doubtful. I am honored to have them included in this book, which has now come to be.

Marie lives in Ellison Bay, Wisc, most of the year, noting that she, *no longer works at The Clearing but it's still in my heart.*

Albert DeGenova

Foreword

This is not a posthumous publication of Norbert Blei's writing. In fact, this is not the book Norbert Blei had intended to write about The Clearing at all. We will never read that book.

The Professor's Quarters is a book inspired by a teacher and completed by his students.

The Clearing Folk School is where Norbert taught a weeklong writing workshop every summer for nearly 40 years. The school, built by landscape architect Jens Jensen, is situated atop one of the most beautiful bluffs in Door County. This is Norbert's Door County, the subject of much of his writing. As with his Clearing book and other unwritten words, all any of us who knew Norb as a person and writer can say is "gone too soon."

Nearly two years prior to his death, Norb invited some of his long-time students to contribute essays to "The Clearing Book" (his working title) and had described it to us with these words:

I am in the midst of devoting some serious time on a book about The Clearing (a teacher's perspective) and invite you to be a part of it. This has long been a desire of mine since I began teaching writing there in the early 1970's.

Bear in mind this is not about me, so much as the place, the course, the people...your sense of self as a student, a writer...how you found your way to Ellison Bay – the clearing in the woods, on a bluff that Jens Jensen created and preserved for you there. What any or all of this may have contributed (continues to contribute) to your life.

I was one of those lucky students asked to write an essay. I understood my teacher; I understood the assignment. But as I began to write about my Clearing experience I quickly realized there was no way I could separate Norbert Blei from The Clearing.

Sadly, on April 23, 2013, Norbert died. So many phone calls, so many reminiscences between the friends I couldn't separate in my memory from Norb and The Clearing. I decided to share my Clearing essay with everyone via a post to my website.

Over the following days, one essay after another traveled via email between Norb's students. Everyone shared their "Clearing Book" assignment, for some the last assignment from their beloved teacher. And, as Norb had envisioned, each essay carried a deeply

Foreword

personal perspective. No two stories were alike, but each essay was similar in its debt to The Clearing and Norbert Blei.

Teacher and place. Inseparable.

We all felt that this book needed to exist not only for those who had contributed their words and experience, but also for anyone in search of a place, a means, to discover themselves. The Clearing is just such a place. Norbert Blei was just the right teacher.

The one person who knew intimately how important this book would have been to Norb is Jude Genereaux. Jude put together an editorial team, dug through email files and Norb's cryptic notes, queried Norb's publisher, searched out all the essays and students, and found the artwork Norb had intended for the book. Thus began the project you now hold in your hands.

There are no drafts, no outlines of what Norb had intended to say in his Clearing book, nor any of his perspectives on being a teacher. There is nothing but the words of his students. But Norb knew what he wanted his Clearing book to be. This is how he described it in a personal email to Jude Genereaux:

And this is a book about love. To write is to love...and one lives to write.

Teacher and place. Inseparable. We hope that in these words you will share our love and experiences at The Clearing Folk School and The Norbert Blei Writing Workshop.

Susan O'Leary

Introduction

Norbert Blei chose for his final public words in this life the inscription on his tombstone: "Find me in my books." And he is there. In his gratitude for the season of solitude in *Winter Book*. The flat out fun of *Paint Me a Picture/Make Me a Poem*. In his love for Chicago in the interviews of *Chi Town* and short stories in *Neighborhood*. In what he called "the beauty and bitching" of *Meditations on a Small Lake*.

But equally, Norb is to be found in his effect on others, especially his students. Norb left formal teaching in 1968. But over his decades of yearly classes at The Clearing, Norb the teacher slowly gathered around him students who came to see themselves as writers because of Norb, who wrote better because of Norb, and who grew into a group of artistic friends, only because of Norbert Blei. Many of us feel that he quite simply changed our lives and that we are who we are now in no small part because of him.

We find him in his books. We find him, too, in the memory we each carry of Norb in his classes in The Clearing Schoolhouse, at his teaching table piled high with books – often first editions - he would and wouldn't get to that week. Filtered light from the bay passed through the cathedral windows behind him, framing his strong presence, as he sat at that simple aged wooden table. We all see him there and hear his resonant bass voice as year after year, the week began.

Photo by Bobbie Krinsky

Introduction

Norbert taught us about the importance of time and space in good writing. Of time and place. And so we see him, too, in his impromptu office in the Professor's Quarters, the plain bayside bedroom that he never slept in but instead kept for his methodical piles of papers and his meetings with us. The meetings we looked forward to and sometimes dreaded. Norb in his high-backed wooden chair at his small corner table, each of us in turn on our chair facing him, knee to knee, as we looked over our work that Norb had read for this meeting. His words were almost always spare, his comments limited. He would show what he liked with a line he had drawn down the margin, a star added quickly next to it for pieces or sections that ranked higher or showed promise. He said so little (we always wanted more), and yet from those meetings, book projects began. "You've got something going here. Write more. It might be a book for Cross+Roads." The conversations always seemed to run over and be late, other writers waiting outside the door, but it was usually because Norb (who read more books and more writers than anyone I have ever known), led you to authors he thought you should read, authors whose writing could influence yours. We would take notes. We would walk out with purpose.

Master teachers introduce you to yourself. In Norb's usual way of saying little about our writing in those individual meetings, he turned us back to ourselves. In asking us questions we weren't sure we had answers for, he pointed us to the path and then left it to us to set out on it.

But we were never alone. The other place we remember and think of Norb is in his chicken coop, his writer's home maybe three hundred feet from his house where he took himself six days a week, every morning, every week, every year for decades until ill health intervened. From his desk in front of the coop window he would write us emails, respond to emails and in earlier days, craft letters and cards. In the written word, somehow he gave us more. It's here he told us things were damn good, showed excitement about our prospects, signed with love. As friend, when times in our lives were dark, he always encouraged with words you held on to.

None of Norb's writers write alike, and this is no small thing. In those Clearing classes, when we would read our work aloud, you knew Jackie's voice, Julie's, Edith's, Kris's, Ralph's, Sharon's, Catherine's, Maja's, Don's. Laurie's, Cheryl's, Sue's, Candace's, Jeannie's. Paula's, Gloria's. As we kept coming back year after year, you knew that no matter the topic Norb gave us to write on, there would be a particular style to each writer. That can be rare in writing teachers, writing programs – that their students each sound so different. But as an extraordinary teacher, Norb taught us to become ourselves and to find the words and cadences that showed who we were.

If at times seeming larger than life, Norb, like the rest of us, was human. He could hold a grudge with impressive obstinacy. But the other side of that resolute stubbornness was an incalculable generosity. In Buddhist teachings the first and foundational of the six perfect understandings is generosity. A life lived just in generosity is a life well lived. And that was Norb as a teacher, not only with us, but also with people he had never met. He responded to letters out of the blue with detail and encouragement. His blogs led to correspondences with farflung readers – a beginning writer in Africa; a soldier existentially cut off in Afghanistan for whom Norb's blog, poetrydispatch was a lifeline. He found time, too, to have coffee with the visitor to Door who had tentatively called, hoping to be a writer, hoping for advice. Norb valued his human connection to each, and found great enduring pleasure in the act of giving.

If we attend to who we are, that self over years may become a honed presence with clear meaning, and we thus simply have the same thing to share over and over again. So we learned from Norb that place tells you who you are – stop to notice that. (It was there all along in the titles of his books.) Words, writers and friends tell you who you are. Listen, read and dig deep. And with a skeptic's reverence for what is beyond the strictly human, Norb taught us, too, to be present for the intangible.

Find him in his books. But find him, too, in a life that penetratingly touched so many others. We each in our way thank you, Norb.

Julie Eger

"Cleared-Away" Space

I drove into The Clearing, a place I had never heard of until a week before, in a car I had never driven before. A 1990 Buick. An old car by current standards, but new to me. None of the levers or knobs were where they were supposed to be. So different from my truck. It was Barbara Vroman's car. She was teaching at The Clearing that fall and she had managed to procure a place for me in her writing class. The campus was full that weekend due to the trees, the leaves in full color, Saturday night.

We followed the road winding back to the campus on the cliffs overlooking the bay, found the parking lot tucked under the trees just as the sun was setting, a pink and magenta halo upon the water. So unlike other campuses I'd seen or heard about. So different than the ones full of cement, blacktop, overhead lights. I had no idea what they meant when they said 'folk school' but I began to form an idea of what this was all about when I entered the cabin and saw the braided wool rug. Rocking chairs. And bookcases filled with the best kind of books, with sturdy spines and nineteenth century fonts embossed in gold and black. Hand-stitched quilts on the beds. Quaint, old-world. It appealed to me.

I woke the next morning to the sound of a bell, a big bell, clanging, clanging. What the hell? Barbara was smiling. "Time to get up. You have 30 minutes until the next bell calls you to breakfast." Breakfast for me was usually coffee, maybe a handful of nuts, a banana. I had no idea how my world was about to change.

I followed Barbara up the steps into a place she called 'the lodge.' There was a buzzing sound coming from inside, voices, laughter and the smell… Oatmeal? Cinnamon? Wafting, welcoming, warm. I didn't know it before I arrived but I realized I had found my way home. A place filled with family-style meals three times a day, and when I looked closely, there were words, words everywhere.

I had found a place to wander down paths that had my name on them, quiet paths full of words and syllables, full of nature, a place littered with creativity around every corner. Paths that led to the workshop. The schoolhouse. The Cliff House. I didn't say much that first time I was there, but I listened a lot. I found out how to get my name on the list to spend a night at The Cliff House with the cedar twig in the door, to keep good spirits

"Cleared-Away" Space

in and bad spirits out. I dragged the sleeping bag inside the tiny cabin built into the side of the cliff and used my flashlight to see as I found the matches, lit the candles, the fire. I threw open the windows with no screens and felt the rush of wind from across the bay. It was autumn and there were no bugs. It was easy to breathe here. It was warm so I let the fire die down. I made a wish and slept with the window wide open all night and dreamed of Jens Jensen and Mertha Fulkerson dreaming up this place.

    Before this I had spent countless hours planning to escape from civilization, somehow, to a place where I could hear the voices of the characters in my head, to write down their stories, and here, people understood that kind of quiet. After all this was The Clearing. A place to clear one's head and heart. Here were old souls, whispering souls, let-me-tell-you-a-story souls. They understood the power of not interrupting someone who was thinking, listening when the characters were ready to speak. Or was it just the land, the waves, the paths, the air that gave birth to such silence?

    The next year I signed up for Norbert Blei's writing class. Everyone knew who Norb was, I thought, except me. They said he was good, the best. He was the one who could show you where the stories were, the ones buried inside you, the ones hidden in the bark of the trees, in the rustle of leaves, in the splash of waves against the rocks, in the shssh of the sawdust under your feet, the sawdust on the paths of The Clearing, the paths that led to everywhere, everywhere your mind could take you.

    And who were these people in his class, these writers? I didn't know anyone, but I fell in love with Ralph Murre's poems, with Susan's meditative walks, Alice's trees and Jackie's straight-forward stories. Where I came from, I wasn't even sure men could read, and here were men shifting words from one sentence to another looking for the right rhythm, setting them in straight lines like the bricks my father laid in straight rows.

    Women were baring their souls without shame, with laughter even. I was terrified that my paltry stories wouldn't fit in, that I wouldn't bare enough of my soul or that I would bare too much. I didn't know the rules, the faces, the big words. But my hand kept moving across the blank pages in my notebook as Norb repeated, "Write about your neighborhood where you grew up," even though I couldn't recall a neighborhood. When I was little I had never lived next-door to anyone. I lived across the field, across the prairie. Was that the same? We didn't interact with people, I hardly knew their names. Should I make something up? I remembered we had room on the prairie, wide open space where the wind blew, with nothing to stop it save some loblolly-like pines on the northeast corner. The wind blew the sand into every crevice, in the house, in our clothes, in the food. We had a lot of crevices but not too many books.

I remember we had plenty of men. With tractors and cows and stuff they planted in the dirt, expected it to grow. And most times it did. It was a hard life full of work that didn't end, work that took time, lots of time. We had as much time as we had wind. But who would want to read about that?

Apparently these people wanted to hear these kinds of stories. They wanted to share their stories. They folded their hands, leaned in on their elbows, closed their eyes, nodded their heads. They smiled and breathed in, breathed in the words. I finally understood the clearing was the first step. Cleaning out the cobwebs, the limiting beliefs, the chaos of a society gone mad. The next step was to let the new ideas slide into the cleared-away space. Ideas one could apply to poems, to stories. Ideas one could apply to life and in doing so, change everything.

Albert DeGenova

Jensen's Great Poem

I'm looking at a black & white photo of the inside of Jens Jensen's Cliff House. In this photo I can smell aged wood and stone, red embers in the hearth, time. I hear the sound of leaves in conversation with the wind and the sighs of the water far below, lapping with each breath of the Lake; the gulls, always the cawing gulls, soar with motionless wings; one fly buzzes against the window pane.

I took this photo in June of 1996, my first visit to The Clearing, and on the small table in this photo is the book I was reading, *The Rag and Bone Shop of the Heart*, an anthology of poetry for men. I remember my first step into the Cliff House, I remember the poems I wrote there that week. I didn't know that I was searching, but when I undid the latch and opened the wood-planked door, I knew I had found it. Sanctuary, solitude, silence, the holy place Jensen built for himself at the far corner of The Clearing property, far from the dining room, the schoolhouse, the energy of students and family, a place seemingly suspended in space, at the edge of a stone bluff, at the far edge of a cultivated world. I remember the journey through that book of poetry sitting at Jens' handmade table. I can look at this photo and bring myself back to the place, like a mantra, a prayer, a centering meditation, a balancing of myself. The Clearing.

For me, discovering The Clearing was discovering Norbert Blei. A visit to Door County at Easter each year had become my family's tradition. Each year we would welcome spring in Door; it became our "new year" celebration. The weekend consisted mostly of hiking, indoor swimming with my two young sons and rummaging through Pastime Books and Caxton's Books. In '94 or '95, I bought a copy of Norb's book, *Meditations on a Small Lake*. So taken with his writing and aesthetic, I uncharacteristically wrote a fan letter to the author, asking where I could buy more of his books and whether he ever taught workshops in the Chicago area. He answered saying I could buy any of his books directly from him and that he taught a writing course each summer. He included a Clearing brochure.

I have been a professional writer since 1979 when I began my working life as a journalist; that was followed by a move into public relations and then into marketing communications. I always say that what I do for a living is marketing, but what I am is a writer.

Jensen's Great Poem

I have also written poetry since high school. With my handful of poetry journal publications, a 1992 self-published chapbook, and my work as a writer, I was accepted into the "advanced" section of the Norbert Blei Writing Workshop.

At that time I had been struggling with my poetry. I had no peer group, no direction, nothing but rejections from journals and a fear of venturing out into the Chicago "poetry scene." I had no idea if my poetry had any value, but I knew that I was driven by something I couldn't explain to continue writing poems. All my creative urges, all my emotional experiences good and bad, came out in lines and sounds of words.

I needed that class, that getaway from life, desperately. My life was in crisis — fracturing around me for all the reasons that sound clichéd — that sound like life — and I needed to escape into poetry, into a writing class. That's what I thought about as I drove from Chicago to Ellison Bay, leaving the people, the traffic, the family, the density and intensity of the city behind. I lit a cigar, turned up the CD player and drove…alone, me and a backpack full of books and an electric typewriter.

Norb's class was everything I had expected…a group of fine writers, poets mostly, good friends with each other, a cohesive, supportive, accepting group that talked about writing and poetry and life as writers, and they accepted me, liked my poetry, asked me to read for them. I had become part of something, but there is only one Norbert Blei. He was the glue, the central energy of the group. His passion for the literary subjects he chooses to teach, his dedication to the writing life, to the purity of the word, to the flow of feeling to thought to words on the page…his stubborn adherence to ideals and perfection…these are what inspire his students, a special kind of student that only needs to stand near the fire to find personal ignition. And a powerful fire Norb is, though he never burns. He does not tell his students what to do, how to fix, what to change; he makes suggestions, offers writing prompts, sends you down the right path…no matter what the path may be for a given student. Most writers in the class know their path (or simply have yet to recognize it); Norb is the torch that throws light upon it, making those next steps clear. The path is always ahead and never out of view.

Outside the schoolhouse and the dorms and the main lodge are the trails, the sunsets, the beach. I'm a city kid to my marrow, a saxophone player with a jazz and blues soundtrack constantly in my head, but I've always felt the call of Lake Michigan, always felt something calling from the waves and always needed to breathe with the wind. This was what I hadn't expected at my first class at The Clearing — walking the trails, finding my special places to sit and view the lake and her sunsets. For the first time in a very long time, I was spending time with myself. And I was writing!

Albert DeGenova

In hindsight, I cannot say which had the strongest effect: Norb, my fellow students, or The Clearing. What I do know is that when I got home from my first Norbert Blei class, I said to myself, out loud at my desk, "I am a poet."

Now, eighteen years later, with four books of poetry to my credit (one of them published by Norb Blei's Cross+Roads Press), I'm also the publisher and co-editor of the literary journal *After Hours*, which I launched in June, 2000. I've performed my poetry throughout the Midwest and I host poetry events in Chicago. I've returned to The Clearing and Norb's classes many times; I can't even begin to express my gratitude to my Clearing friends, lifelong and dear. I was Norb's assistant teacher in 1999 and 2000; and again helped lead the class in 2008 and 2009. I've learned that I love to teach writing and poetry as well. In fact, I missed The Clearing in 2003-2005 when I was working on my MFA in writing. I can say unequivocally that it was my first visit to The Clearing in June, 1996, when my path was suddenly lit and became ever so clear. (And today, after Norb's passing in 2013, together with Susan O'Leary, I am now leading The Norbert Blei Writing Workshop... keeping his legacy alive.)

I am looking at a black & white photo of the inside of Jens Jensen's Cliff House. It hasn't changed. This year, 2011, I spent the night there (again). A restful, peaceful night with a roaring fire that sang me to sleep. Years ago, overnighting in the Cliff House was fearful, was learning how to be completely alone. But it is from this kind of solitude that art is born. Some find it in dirty attics or musty basements; there was a time when I could find solitude on a city bus or a crowded cafeteria, but today, I find it among the beech and birch trees, the quiet Lady Slippers and exploding poppies, in the cedar sprigs I rub in my hands to inhale the musk of mother nature. This is where I refocus the poetry inside me.

Now, as I hike through The Clearing, I know that I am walking through Jens Jensen's great, living work of art. The trees have grown up as he planned, the vistas open up just as he intended. This landscape, the world in its natural state, untamed vines, mosses, wildflowers growing as they will, bats darting through the dark, jagged tree trunks split by wind and lightning makes The Clearing Jensen's great poem, wild and free in its phrasing and emotion, but crafted by a man's vision, a poem that lends its meaning to each reader's interpretation, to each reader's need.

My annual Clearing. Empty the everyday, empty the unbalanced soul, and you are filled with your own truths. I am filled with my own meaning once again and returning to my life I can say, "I am a poet."

Legacy

On a summer day in 1972, I drove the winding road into The Clearing for the first time, not as a student, but as a librarian on a mission. A few years earlier Leonard Eaton, author of *Landscape Artist in America: The Life and Work of Jens Jensen*, had come to the Morton Arboretum where I worked, talked about his book, and left us with a big box of archival materials. This became the seed for the Sterling Morton Library's Jens Jensen Collection, and cataloging those papers set me on a path that would change my life.

Now here I was at The Clearing, to see what might be added to our collection. With me was my friend, Orvetta Robinson, librarian at the Illinois State Museum, who had been to The Clearing many times and was concerned about the scattered papers she knew were there. All week we approached our task with a joyous fever, delving into every cupboard, drawer, closet, attic, cellar, and cubbyhole. We unearthed letters, clippings, paintings, landscape plans, and photos, and we shared the excitement of our finds with students and staff. We took time to walk the bluff trail, descend to the Cliff House, test the water at the beach, and visit with Sid Telfer and Miss Emma Toft. I couldn't have had a better guide than Orvetta, and as the ambience of this serene and special place seeped into my soul, I knew I would be back.

Jensen's papers did go to the Arboretum, and Orvetta and I came to The Clearing again the next summer to inventory historic arts and artifacts. Thus began my several decades of association with the Friends of The Clearing. But my first class at The Clearing was "Writing" with Norbert Blei, June 15-21, 1975.

It was Sunday evening when fifteen strangers met around the tables in the dimly lit dining room, expecting to be taught how to write or write better. And Norb – so endearingly grizzled in later years that I can hardly remember how he looked then – was there to gently nudge us toward writerhood. He began with the fundamental notion that poetry is the basis of all good writing. "Think of three one-word poems." (Thunderclouds? Serendipity? Whisper? Do those count?) As students shared their words, we began to know each other.

"What is writing about?" Norb enlightened us: "Discipline, writing something every day." "Be aware of material around you, including yourself." "A quiet way of life . . . communicating to yourself . . . clarifying things in your own mind." "Constant discovery."

Each day, he nurtured us onward: "The way to do is to be." "Don't explain, suggest." "Make it sing!" "Pare it down." "Find new ways of saying things." And there were assignments: "Make a poem." ("Pioneer," about my great-aunt Sue.) "Think of 13 ways of looking at something." (I chose Fire!) "Interview someone in the class." (Bill Stipe, who persuaded us there is no sunrise, only ETSA – earth turns, sun appears.) We retreated to our own special places to write, then came to class to expose our efforts, reading our work aloud, listening, responding, reflecting. Norb commented, sometimes reading to us, including his own work.

We delved deep and reached out. We whispered in dorms while others slept. Twosomes talked side-by-side on the stone walls. We drew up wooden lawn chairs for spacious conversations. Non-stop chatter raised the noise-level in the dining room, and quieter thoughts were shared along the narrow, root-fraught high bluff trail. We were finding the away-ness, the simplicity, the silence, the community, the reflection, and the clearing-away that this place offered. Jensen's magic was working.

Then came Friday– all too soon! Time to finish, tie up loose ends. What had we accomplished? Who did we need to spend last precious moments with? And what could we think up for the "Friday night program?"

After supper we made our way to the Schoolhouse and settled in. Norb talked, we all talked. Finally, we presented our crazy skit, "The Twelve Days of Writing." Betsy led off, singing "On the first day of writing our teacher said to us. . ." and we sang back, "The way to do is to be!" On it went, as we called Norb poet, writer, captain, philosopher, eggman, da slovak, tutor, maestro, and guru, each of us singing one of his gifts: "Poetry is the basis of all good writing," "Always be aware," "Less is more," "Did you ever really look at an egg?" "Fragments, I want fragments," "I hope you won't use any clichés," "Put yourself in every story," "Without humor there is no hope." We had a hilarious time!

Next morning we said our goodbyes and drove away. It was hard to go home, and I wondered if I would see any of these new friends again. Before long a postcard came from Nancy. "Dear Egg Ladies," she began (referring to Norb's Egg Lady story), inviting several of us to an overnight at her home in Kohler. And so we "gathered," talking, laughing, and snacking far into the night. After that we met at least once a year, often at the beach to share book-talk, gossip, writings, food, laughter, and losses. And we began giving each other

Legacy

chicken-y things, whimsical tokens just for fun. Our houses were full of these by the summer of 2010, when five of us met to celebrate our thirty-fifth year together: Nancy Ellrodt, Grace Howaniec, Betsy Michael, Alice Randlett, and myself.

Jens Jensen believed that environments have a profound effect on people, and surely he created just such an environment at The Clearing. For me the effect has been bountiful in many ways, but most of all in a richness of friendships – countless members of the Friends; Jensen scholars and Jensen descendants; the radical centenarian Ann Markin, avid Clearing student of the 1950s and '60s; and the extraordinary modern dancer Sybil Shearer, Jensen's friend for whom he built The Clearing's dance ring, and whose foundation I now serve as a trustee. Not to mention the Egg Ladies and Norbert Blei. Oh, my. Who could imagine so fine a legacy?

Sue Wentz

Fertile Ground

There was a flower.

No, let me back up.

On the porch of The Clearing's Main Dorm—a lovely rustic cabin—there was a flower. In the interests of full disclosure, it might have been a weed. I'm not well versed in such things. Nevertheless, from a tiny crack in a rock within the porch's foundation, a slender shoot emerged, its stem softly curving upward to a delicate yellow blossom.

Amidst the early June splendor of Door County in general and The Clearing in particular, the ambitions of one upstart flower should hardly have been worth the notice. Now, over ten years later, it still seems a strange detail for my memory to hold onto with such insistence. But somehow, that tiny yellow blossom perhaps best represents The Clearing's lasting impact on my life—and on my emergence—as a writer.

Much like that seed wedged deep in the stone by wind or rain, I did not enjoy the luxury of good soil or abundant sunlight in either my personal or creative life. I came to Norbert Blei's creative writing class at The Clearing truly uncertain about both my ability and my worth. I felt I did not belong among people who were surely talented, established, and successful. I didn't have a track record of publishing credits or success stories. All I could offer was my desire to learn. I wasn't sure that was enough.

But there is something about the place. Even a seed in a rock finds fertile ground. Every morning I explored the trails that wound through the woods, skirting past meadows and along the bluff overlooking Ellison Bay. Some of the pathways were wide and impeccably groomed. Others were less well delineated. No matter. I walked. I listened to the heartbeat of wind and waves, and took the pulse of a quieter world. I found the air and began to breathe.

From that foundation, I mustered up the courage to poke my head above the surface. In the classroom, under the nurturing of Blei's calm encouragement, I felt myself begin to reach and stretch as a writer. When my fellow students took turns reading their own

Fertile Ground

assignments aloud, it fell like summer rain; every drop unique and nourishing.

Rubbing elbows and passing dishes in the dining room, or sharing the fruits of our creative labors in the Lodge on a rainy afternoon, I saw the same sort of growth in my new friends. Some exploded into bloom, bright and breath-taking. Others were softer, more serene, but we all blossomed from whatever seeds we had brought with us. We made quite the bouquet.

And no matter what soil we came from, we put down roots here. We tangled them into lifelong friendships and forever memories of person, of teacher, and certainly of place.

At The Clearing, we had all found fertile ground.

Even that tiny yellow flower.

Kristen Thacher

The Writing Life

Writers Workshop. The Clearing. 2004.
    Can poetry save a life? My mother and I travel together to The Clearing for Norbert Blei's Writers Workshop. I am 56 and wondering about the whole of my life, not just wondering if I am a writer. My eighty-four year old mother is wondering how to fit her life stories onto 8 x 11 sheets of paper. A lot of expectations for a week at a folk school.
    The Clearing is a land-locked island surrounded by deep evergreen pools and sun-flecked waves of meadow grass frothing with wildflowers. Secret places. Thoughtful places. When we drive past the stone entry pillar, down a winding dirt road, the outside world disappears for six days. Sanctuary.
    My mother is a beginner; and I must begin again. We both write and rewrite. We read to one another at night in our shared room. My mother is better at the telling; I am better at writing it down. We pick and choose our words. Norb suggests, "The poet expresses the impossible by suggesting." We revise again. Everyone at the Writers Workshop —writers, teachers, guest speaker— talks about the importance of keeping journals and about harvesting those journals for other writing projects.
    My mother's storytelling is a living journal. My handwritten journals take on a new aspect. It's as if the journals are poor people in India who have no jobs and need to sell their internal organs to wealthy Westerners requiring transplants. If I expose my bleeding innards, what will you pay me? Will you survive the transplant? Will I survive the loss? The excision of publication. To be published is the most sought after and most elusive goal. Does publication mean my words are in a better arrangement than yours? The big publishing houses want a best seller; but not everyone writes to that bottom line. So many voices will never be heard. So why do I keep writing poetry? Not for the money. Then Norb reminds us, "It all starts with poetry."

Writers Workshop. The Clearing. 2005.
    Ceremony and Ritual. Lightning strikes the dead Ponderosa next to my house a day before I leave for The Clearing. In New Mexico, unrelenting drought and forest fires have threatened to turn me and my memories into ashes before we can escape. I move

The Writing Life

favorite books, photographs, art work, and the journals down off the mountain to a concrete storage unit in town. History. Why do I need the written words, need to put my hands on the story? Memoir and memory. Words and objects are reminders. In 24 hours, I evacuate my poems and myself, fly across the country, join my mother, head north and finally arrive in Door County just before dusk. We toast one another with champagne at a restaurant as the last of the sunset reflects on Lake Michigan. We've made it back. Back to the water.

A few days later at the Clearing in the Schoolhouse, I take a seat in the loose circle of my new old friends, who ask me, how was your year? No one had hinted that the Writers Workshop and The Clearing would change me radically. I tell them. I have quit my jobs and opened a new pottery studio. I have achieved enough momentum to escape standard orbit. I have walked back into the invisible stream, strong currents that push you outward and pull you back. It is the same river, and it is not the same. I am on the journey again. I work the whole week on the Drought Poems that I have found in myself. I search through the past year's notes, poems jotted down in parking lots on the backs of envelopes, phrases written on the side of the road on old shopping lists, fragments scrawled at midnight on the telephone notepad next to the bed, a clutter of post-its handy for printing on the dashboard. My dedicated writing space seems to be my car.

I sort out all the pieces into small stacks on the squares of the handmade quilt on my bed at the Clearing. Where do I start? Here. Where do I end? At the next beginning. Mother doesn't know where to start either. She is advised to write down her favorite stories rather than one long narrative starting at the beginning of her life. The events will sort out into the whole. She tells me a story from her career as a WAVE in World War II, and I ask her about the particulars. In telling me, she remembers details she has left out. I practice reading my long poem about the drought out loud and Mom coaches me: slow down, enunciate, breathe. On Friday night at the reading in the Schoolhouse, I'm surprised by applause. Then a few weeks later, there's a note from Norb: "Get back to me with the Drought Poems. Send me what you've got. Damn it, woman, you're a poet! Keep 'em coming!" Norb hints, there may be a book in the works. But, he admonishes, the unnamed book is a closely guarded secret. Don't tell. Undisclosed destinations. Suspect terrain. Superstition.

Writers Workshop. The Clearing. 2006.

Putting It All Together. My poetry and pottery share the same visions and metaphors. Each Drought Poem is protected in its own clay cylinder, like the Dead Sea Scrolls hidden in clay jars in a desert cave. I have printed out each of the poems on handmade paper, then rolled the paper up in a scroll, tied closed with twine, and hidden in a stoneware pot patterned with bark beetle scribings from dead pinyon branches. Words on paper, or electronic computer files, words so easily destroyed by fire or flood or passing time. How can I preserve my words? Should I memorize and recite, like Mother's storytelling? Today, tomorrow, or in 30,000 years, will the story or the poem be the same?

The poems are like an art show. It's a snapshot of a moment. By the time everyone sees the show or reads the poems, the artist is long gone into the next creation. Writing, for the writer, is not just the finished piece, it is an unending revelation. The artist learns not to be dependent on outside criticism or praise; the writer wonders at being understood. Mom reads her tale about taking a Soviet admiral on a tour of Norfolk Harbor in 1944. Many have forgotten the Russians were our supposed allies at that time. One young woman tries to correct what she thinks is my mother's error. No danger of revisionism there. My mother knows what happened to her in 1944. She sets the young woman straight. I perform my words, give voice to my poem, at the Friday night reading in the Schoolhouse. At the end, silence. Silence can be as loud, laudatory as applause. Words that you speak are written in a different cadence than words that are written to be read in silence. The Living Word. The nuances of stories we tell one another out loud may change with the storyteller. The stories that we write down are set, constrained by the boundaries of each letter and by time. The words cannot change. Only the reader changes.

The Writing Life. The Clearing. 2007.

You will never forget. That first time. It's like nothing else that will ever happen in your life. The time and place framed forever. Just as in the old stories, the ugly duckling suddenly swans up into the air and away. No going back. And just when you think you have finally accepted the idea that the writing life is a journey, not a destination, you arrive at a pleasing place and think you might like to get off the road. It all comes down to a single book, an anthology with your name on the back cover, in crisp black and white, with all the other writers. Just like that, the snake sheds its skin. I am a published poet. Transformation. No turning back.

I cannot wipe the smile from my face, or the worry from my mind. What have I done? Hard copy. No deniability. Manifestation. My thoughts, in words, for anyone to read. Visions and metaphors so carefully crafted that there are not many secrets left here. Confirmation. No more anonymity, no more low profile, no more traveling in the desert after dark. *Other Voices*, edited by Norbert Blei, published by Cross+Roads Press, Ellison Bay, Wisconsin. In the first workshop, Norb had warned us, "We're here for a moment. The writing career is long and wide." Norb, editor and publisher, testifies in the preface: "Real writing is what we need to know ourselves…Art matters. Good writing can change lives."

Susan O'Leary

Mr. Blei

When Norb's writers passed our chapters among ourselves after he died, I shared my last letter to Norb, the one I wrote a few days before his expected death, thanking him a final time. My chapter is based on that letter rather than the piece I had originally sent Norb for the book.

I was the lucky one who met Norbert Blei – Mr. Blei – in 1965 when I was fifteen years old and his student in a suburban Chicago high school. He was young then, in his late twenties. He wore corduroy jackets with leather patches on his elbows and carried a pipe. He would enter the room, his fingers circling the handles of his large beat up leather briefcase, and empty its contents on the desk – much like he did at The Clearing – of more books than we the students were reading. And then he would begin.

We were enthralled. He taught two honors sections of English II, small classes with maybe 10 or 12 students each. I've counted up now, and close to a quarter of us ended up in Ivy League schools. We were the best the villages of LaGrange and LaGrange Park and Western Springs had to offer, and he gave us F's if he didn't think we were taking seriously the necessity of pushing ourselves to learn. To be more. At the beginning of the school year, he took us to an exhibit of student art work and told us to write about it right there at the exhibit. The next day he tore apart the five paragraph essays most had written, reminding us that art is to enter into, not respond to conventionally through a safe distance. Many F's that day. We began to wake up.

He said to suburban teenagers in the early 1960's, "Here's Richard Wright, here's James Joyce, here are Albert Camus and Gwendolyn Brooks – what are you going to do with them?" We had never known there were books or ideas like this. Starting with them we found more.

I fell in love with words with Mr. Blei. With freedom, on the page and in thought. He had us keep journals in spiral notebooks a good decade before they became commonplace in high school classes, and collected them every few weeks to read. I didn't have a clue what free verse was, but I moved into it without thinking, because of the way that words opened up with him. I remember how we waited for him to return our notebooks, the same

Mr. Blei

lines and stars in the columns of what we had written that Clearing students later recognized as his way of reading work. Sophomores who had always excelled in school but not necessarily thought closely about things, we saw ourselves a second time through his eyes, came to value a potential we hadn't known we had. I remember the script of how I formed letters then – that changing, too, in that year with him, because words didn't fit quite right anymore in how I had written them.

With the world of the mind opening to me through Mr. Blei, I started traveling on the Burlington to Chicago, leaving the train station and walking each time straight down city-center blocks toward the lake until I turned on Wabash Avenue for Kroch and Brentano's and their books in the basement – the underground books. I brought home City Lights' titles and a growing collection of poetry. I read more Joyce, understanding almost nothing, but moving larger because of having read him. I regularly climbed alone the stone steps to the Art Institute, because to see art as a beginner, to sit and view color and shape, it felt right to do so in silence and solitude. But even absent, he sat there with me on those gallery benches, telling me, "This can be yours. This can be yours."

I believed him, and he simply changed my life.

Mr. Blei left the Chicago area for Door County two years later, but we stayed in touch when I was in college, through letters, and night visits to the city when he and I were both back in town to see family. The conversations in car rides and walks on the north side – our routine usually eventually taking us to Lower Wacker Drive - were looser because we had moved now into friendship and now he was Norb to me. He had a way of asking a question that turned a conversation into specificity, took it to a deeper level and so, as we walked or sat in restaurants, we talked for hours. One time in July in the summer of 1971 I had a new Pentax SLR camera, and we shot a roll of film – capturing the Wrigley building lit up against dark sky, the detail of the Michigan Avenue Bridge, ourselves in midnight urban light.

And then for years, as we each raised families and money was thin both ways, we stayed in touch only through letters. Which grew further apart.

I found Norb again when I finally let myself come to The Clearing in the late nineties for his particular method and life in books. I had known the Chicago Norb. Here I came to know him through his connection to the land and his absolute love for The Clearing, rooted in his sureness of the importance of place. Of this *particular* place – the meadow, the woods, the shore, Jens Jensen's space for mind and body. Buildings created from the stone surrounding them. Paths along the shore that had been walked for hundreds of years before immigrant settlers, that we now walked, too. Landscape architecture that respected what this particular land and its indigenous plants and trees taught.

People and place. That is what fundamentally The Clearing brings together. And Norb the journalist with *who, what, when, where* and *why* in his bones taught us here the importance of the setting in telling who a person is – a setting the reader can see and believe, want to enter into. He pushed us to remember the detail of where we came from, to find the detail of where we were. And to situate it all in time, in era, in belief.

The summer Norb asked me to assist him in his next year's Beginner Class I sat in to watch it each day as he taught. 'The Interview' was always on Thursday, and each year Norb would ask a different student from the Advanced Class to come down to the Schoolhouse at the end of the morning to be interviewed by the beginners. I remember to this day watching how he physically leaned into the topic of how to ask a question. He knew this with instinct and nuance and purpose. He explained there is a subtlety to listening for voice shift in tenor and timber, to recognizing small changes in a person's face that help you to understand when you are getting to the heart of a topic and a soul. He modeled how to pause, how to ask a little closer. He was teaching so much more than writing. Sitting there I understood I was watching how he found the material for the Blei feature articles that many Chicagoans in the 60's and 70's came to search out each week in the *Chicago Tribune Sunday Magazine*, and that later were collected into *Neighborhood* and *ChiTow*n. Norb wrote looking for and recognizing life; what it is to be human.

I also realized I was watching a master teacher at his best. Most of the writing students who were in this very moment conducting the interview had never imagined they would do this – interview in order to truly know more. And they were tentative. Yet somehow as Norb guided them, his words were both entryway and refinement. I kept imagining as I was watching him that two sets of words were coming out of his mouth at the same time – one introducing the form of the interview, one delving into the nuance of the interview with experienced writers – and yet these very different meanings were both inherent in the simple words he was speaking and in the care that was a part of the way he offered them. The clarity and exactness of what he said were the qualities of the haiku that Norb so dearly loved; his words acted almost as image, which was why they could be taken in with multiple meanings. A teacher myself, I was changed in that hour of sitting there, watching Norb teach.

I was now in my forties, then fifties, no longer the teenager Norb first knew. There was an ease and a closeness we both relied on now, and it was there in no small part because of how he had taught me decades before to question and believe in life. We still had our nights out together, but now they were to the AC Tap or maybe Trio. The

Mr. Blei

conversations were about books and friends, life and art.

With his true love of people, it was natural that a group of writers would grow around Norb. I think he knew that it was at The Clearing in Jensen's simple construct of study, nature and common meals that he could help create the friendship of this circle of writers whom I have written with now for almost a quarter of my life. That as we gathered with him, we would learn each other's topic, each other's style and stance. Because of Norb, I know these friends through their words, and because of Jensen and Mertha Fulkerson, I know these friends through this place. Words and land coming together, land holding words as rock holds soil.

Easily twenty of our books have their genesis in the weeks with him and each other at The Clearing.

We tend to forget that Norb, beyond writer and teacher, was painter, too. In different periods of his life the visual arts paralleled or overtook his writing. I think part of Norb's draw to – and at times wrangles with – The Clearing was his deep affinity with Jensen's vision of a place in nature where adults could pause to quietly know themselves and to know art. He felt a particular kinship with the visual and musical artists among us – Kris Thacher for her pottery, Bobbie Krinsky for her photos. And Al for his saxophone, his flute.

Part of what Norb left us was to live art in life. As writers, to find the exact words for it, words that might cause readers to linger in what you just said. Words that at certain times may give you a sense of having done what you wanted to do. Which ultimately, Mr. Blei, Norbert Blei, that rare one among us, did. With words on paper, words in the air.

Maja Jurisic and Don Fraker

Writing at The Clearing with Norb Blei

Since I'm a doctor and my husband is a lawyer, we both spend a fair portion of our professional lives writing. But it's a form of writing that is tethered to facts and data. I had longed to free myself of those constraints for some while, to let my words soar, not dangerously high, but just a bit, on wings of fancy. So, when I saw a writing class listed in the catalogue of a school for adults in Ellison Bay called The Clearing, I persuaded my husband, Don, to come with me: nagging and badgering is, after all, a time-honored form of persuasion in marriage.

Don and I had long enjoyed and faithfully visited Door County for its views (land meeting water, lake meeting sky, and the glories of both sunrise and sunset), galleries, performing arts, and its sprinkling of charming villages. But it wasn't until our experience at The Clearing that we fell in love with the peninsula.

Sure, I'd been to Door County before. Legal conferences and vacations. Bed and breakfasts, biking in Peninsula State Park. Shopping. Our favorite art gallery in the world (Edgewood Orchard). So I went along with my wife's new idea of taking a writing course. At least it wasn't as expensive as some of her other ideas. And even though I wasn't confident I could write without footnotes, I was willing to give it a try.

We actually missed the entrance to The Clearing the first time, obscured from the uninitiated by trees and vegetation. Once we found it, as we drove down the winding lane flanked by trees standing like dutiful sentinels, we sensed that we were truly getting away from the mundane and arriving at a special destination. We passed a meadow, found the unobtrusive parking area tucked into the woods, and walked up a path onto what we now know is called Central Campus. At first sight, it seemed like a charmed village. Wooden cottages and a large stone building were pleasingly arrayed around a courtyard enlivened with the bright orange of tall poppies in full bloom. It was a place out of a storybook.

As we explored the property further, we became even more enamored. So much so, that every year, as soon as we deposit our bags in our assigned cottage, I hurry out to reacquaint myself with the cliff path that goes from The Clearing property all the way into Ellison Bay. I breathe deeply, stop rushing, and relax fully. At this point, we must have over

Writing at The Clearing with Norb Blei

a hundred photos taken on and from that path: rocks seen through clear water from 40 feet up, waves whipped up into a frenzied froth, views of the reassuring bulk of the headlands across the bay. And as I look through the pictures between seasons, I can smell air redolent of pine, feel the wind coloring my cheeks and messing up my hair, and even hear the gulls.

Years after our first Clearing classroom experience, we still remember the moment when we entered the Schoolhouse and encountered that quintessential Teacher, Norbert Blei. Don loves to tell this part.

Entering the rustic schoolhouse, my trepidation at embarking on adult education was heightened by the cathedral-like windows through which light was streaming reverentially down upon our instructor, his backlit fringe of gray-white hair, halo-like, combining with a visage of deep-set, dark-rimmed eyes, and multiple stacks of books and hand-outs on the desk in front of him, imparting the impression that his words would be nothing short of sacred pronouncements.

And who could forget our first in-class assignment? After spending an hour or so talking about the habits of good writers, journaling and the like, and sharing some instructive examples, Norb passed around copies of a photo. It showed a totally unclothed man and woman, full frontal, the man splattered in blood, holding a large bloody knife and the woman touching him lightly on the chest. While my Norwegian-Lutheran eyes were still in the bugging-out stage, we heard Norb's gravelly voice commanding, "Now take ten minutes and tell me whether they're naked or nude." Yow! Footnotes were the furthest thing from my mind now. Time to think, or react, or both, time to start writing.

The Clearing offers many types of classes and several different writing courses. Over time, some instructors have developed a coterie of faithful students, who return year after year. Foremost among these teachers was Norb Blei, and Don and I could be numbered among his groupies. We looked forward to his class every year, not knowing exactly what would be in store, but knowing it would be a week of revelation. We knew that Norb's approach and high expectations would make us better writers, and we could hardly wait to hear what our fellow students had been writing. One of the great joys of being part of this group is that there are some very serious, fine, and productive writers in it. They don't just dabble in writing, but make it a core part of their daily life. Being surrounded by such talented and hard-working people is inspiring. And perhaps because Norb insisted that writers have to dig deep and tell the truth, we felt as if we knew more about the essential natures of our Clearing writing friends than about many of the people we saw most days of the year.

Although reading is one of the passions my husband and I have long shared, Norb introduced us to authors and literature unfamiliar to us. The depth and breadth of his knowledge and appreciation of good writing and writers from all parts of the world was unparalleled. And he asked questions that forced people to think. So, while there are no phones and no TV at The Clearing, there are plenty of enquiring minds engaged in discussion and creation.

The mind is housed in the body, so we would be remiss if we didn't say a few words about the creature comforts and domestic arrangements. A week at The Clearing is as good for your circadian rhythms as it is dangerous for your waistline. Woken by a bell at 7 am, students are served breakfast at 7:30, dinner at noon, and supper at 6 PM. Mealtimes are regular and the meals are regularly feasts. The fact that meals are also served "family style," with everyone sitting at long tables, makes them part of the bonding experience. Sometimes, when I'm coming up the stairs to the lodge where the meals are served, I pause for a few seconds and close my eyes, and just listen to the rise and fall of familiar voices wholeheartedly occupied in conversation. The harmony of the cacophony makes me smile.

The one pronouncement I most remember now from that very first meal at The Clearing is not to sit in the same seat twice. I suppose I could have taken that admonition in the Heraclitean sense and asked, "How could I?" but I chose to interpret it literally and avoid repetitive chair occupancy as if it were a crime punishable by banishment.

As a card-carrying foodie, I'm ashamed to say I can't recall what was served at that first supper. I was too busy making conversation, making strangers into acquaintances, but I did learn not to call that meal dinner (that's the mid-day repast) and I did learn that all food travels clockwise.

Jens Jensen's vision of a place of beauty and unspoiled nature where adults could go to refresh their spirits is an enduring one. Thanks to his efforts, and those of many who shared his dream, The Clearing has survived the twentieth century, and is still there beckoning us, welcoming us, simultaneously stimulating and calming us, standing as a symbol of all that is good and vital to preserve. We feel so lucky that we stumbled upon this charmed and charming place, and can feel part of a community of people who (roughly borrowing from T.S. Eliot) never cease from exploration, and yet at the end of all the exploring, can not only see where they started through clear eyes, but also express it with just the right words.

Jens' Dream Fulfilled

White pillars of birch frame the sawdust paths. Moccasin flowers point their yellow slippers and ribboned tresses from the green undergrowth; the Solomon plume, young ash, beech and birch, the creeping juniper. Here and there, pale blue clouds of forget-me-nots find a niche among the rocks. The vireo asks his eternal question.

On the paths the students walk, scuffling, talking in low voices, reviewing the lesson they have just left. The Janes and Jeans, the Michelles and Amelias, a Robert or Richard or Ted. The birches have watched them pass, year after year; have listened, stretched arms, watched as the lights were put in, interrupting the soft blackness with their gold beams. Squirrels scale the birch trunks, leap from their branches, unsettling the vireos, nuthatches and chickadees.

Perhaps he knew it would be like this – Jens Jensen, the man with a vision who created this unique school. He carved it out of an old farmstead on the top of a bluff, believing that in an environment so blessed, minds would stretch and grow, learning would happen; that those who walked here would absorb an understanding of the value of each twig and leaf, each hum and twitter: the whole of nature, integrated and unspoiled. And it would change them.

I first learned about The Clearing in 1961. We had moved from New York to Wisconsin in 1960, and I was still trying to adjust to the quiet after the clamor and intensity of Manhattan. Our new neighbors in the student rental houses told us they were going to a place called Door County for a weekend, and asked us to come along. The woman, one of the most creative and curious people I would ever know, said there was a place called The Clearing that she wanted to visit – an adult arts school or retreat, she called it.

And so we found it and wandered in one late afternoon in June of 1961. I was immediately enchanted. I don't remember whether there were classes going on, or whether we talked to anyone. It was June, so the poppies must have been blooming; sunshine filtered down on the paths through tall trees. I remember standing in the Lodge and looking out the cathedral window at the three white pines and the lake beyond, and thinking, with a certainty that was deeper than words, I will be back here. We picked up literature and schedules, corralled our rowdy tots and left.

Years went by, as I continued to think about writing, continued to dream story plots and characters while I attended PTA and Little League baseball. Eighteen years.

Then in 1979, a friend who had become an accomplished wood carver was invited to teach a class at the Clearing. She came back full of enthusiasm. I studied the brochure she brought me, and sure enough, there was a writing class. Someone named Norbert Blei was teaching both beginning and advanced writing.

I went to the library and found a copy of *The Hour of the Sunshine Now*, short stories by Norbert Blei. I was captivated by the writing. It was different. The people in the stories came to life in his words, and I knew them. Maybe, I thought, I could learn to write like that. I had always written, always dreamed of being an author since I was in the fourth grade. I signed up for the class and arrived for the first time in June of 1980. Driving into the woods, along the gravel drive, I knew I had made the right decision.

The subject that week was Zen, (and the Art of Writing). I had read the assignments, Alan Watts, and whatever else, and wasn't sure whether I understood them. The first day in class, in the high-ceilinged stone "schoolhouse" with its own tall window, I was tingly as a first grader, eager to plunge in. I loved everything about this place – the hand-carved wood, the rustic tables and chairs. Norbert Blei had long hair and a mustache, a deep and resonant voice and brown eyes full of sparkle, dark with knowing. There was a compelling magnetism about him. He passed out a grammar quiz. Ha, I thought (English major to the core) my chance to shine. I answered all the questions perfectly, smug and self-assured. When we had finished, he said, "Now crumple it up and throw it away. That's not what this class is about."

Then he handed out objects and asked us to describe them - not as they were, but in a metaphorical sense - what were they like? This was different. Other students had more imaginative answers. I was so literal! I struggled. We learned about haiku. Recorded our dreams. I wrote my first poem.

As the week went on, I remember finding a rock niche along the beach, where I could write my haiku, write about dreams, listen to the slapping of waves on limestone. I felt like I had achieved nirvana. I might not have understood completely then, but I came to understand, how Norb's teaching and the setting – Jens' Jensens's Clearing – were in perfect harmony.

Jens' Dream Fulfilled

In the beginners class with me were two writers who became dear friends: Joe Patrick and Peg Nemeth. We read to each other and laughed till our jaws ached. I remember mealtimes, uproarious with Joe's jokes and speculations, meals that stuck to your ribs and filled your belly. Our Friday night readings surprised us all.

After that first week, I packed up and left Saturday morning with a feeling of despair. During the long drive home, my mind seethed with memories and words, spun with possibilities and plots for my next escape. I had needed this week for so long, like a hungry person seeking sustenance. How could I make it last? Could I come back again? I did. Again and again.

In the late 80's, The Clearing went through a crisis when its owner, The Farm Bureau, decided they could not take responsibility any longer. The interests that originally brought them together had diverged, and suddenly The Clearing had to become independent, and self-sustaining, which meant raising a lot of funds. During those years I served on the "Clearing in Transition" Board, and, when we were successful, on the Board of the new, independent The Clearing. A heady time. We knew that this unique place, with its woods, water and cliffs, with its eager students and outstanding teachers, was worth the fight. Many staunch and loyal lovers of The Clearing, led by Tim Stone, spent countless hours of meetings and fundraising to assure its survival. I was fortunate to know many of these people – friends, supporters, and staff – who dedicated themselves so that Jensen's dream would be fulfilled.

Meanwhile, I wrote, and I returned to The Clearing whenever I could. Norb was a constant support, mentor and friend. His notes of encouragement, the clippings, books, criticisms and suggestions were a lifeline. I still have all of them, and my early assignments, with his scrawled comments in the inimitable bold black pen. I remember the day – perhaps 10 years after my first Clearing Class – that I finally wrote to him, "I have decided I am a poet." It was scary and thrilling at the same time.

Because I wrote a lot of nature poems, Norb suggested that I do a whole book about trees. I did, and re-worked it for several years. In 2004, Norb published *A Blessing of Trees* from his wonderful Cross+Roads Press. It won the Posner Prize the following year from the Council for Wisconsin Writers for best book of poems published that year in Wisconsin.

Someone once asked me what it was about Norb that made him such an inspiring teacher. How does he teach you to write? they asked.

And I tried to explain the unexplainable. *He cares passionately about writing and writers*, I said. *He opens your mind to the best writing there is. He makes you believe that he cares about you. He ignites your soul.*

I Am Here

It isn't that I get lost more easily with each passing year. More confused. No, it certainly isn't that. It's just that they – or maybe, we – keep making one place look just like another. The Acura dealer is out past Long John Silver's. Target is next to T.G.I. Friday's. IHOP pushes pancakes at Pleasant Prairie and, probably, Pike's Peak. Oklahoma begins to look like Ohio. You get it; you've been there. It threatens to turn me into a curmudgeon before my time.

Still, I can occasionally find unbeaten paths to places that have maintained their own identities; sometimes for lack of commercial potential, it's true, but sometimes because somebody cared so deeply for these places that they were willing to overlook the possibility of profit. When I find myself in such a spot, I am suddenly not lost at all, not confused. In fact, there is a great and rare clarity. I am HERE!

I followed one such (somewhat unbeaten) path about forty miles north of the last of the big chain outlets, out onto a peninsula in Lake Michigan, to a point near the End of The Earth where lies the embodiment of a dream. The dreamer, fortunately, was Jens Jensen, a man with the ambition and capability to bring substance to his vision. His dream, also fortunately, was to build in integration with nature, that is, into the native wood and stone of the place, rather than upon it. In harmony. Here, there would be a folk school; peer teaching peer, people knowledgeable in all manner of subjects, both scholars and artisans, mentoring one another. I liked the sound of it. The Clearing. I'd go to see if I could get some help with my writing. I'd spend a day or two with Ellen Kort, poet laureate. A week. Susan O'Leary, Zen traveler. The infamous Norbert Blei might take me under his wing. I could hope.

But here's the question: Unless you're particularly interested in becoming a "nature writer" or "nature artist" (and I was not), what's the point of traveling off to such a site, beautiful though it may be, to study? Couldn't you learn the same thing at a workshop at a university, say, or maybe even on-line from some virtual vice-principal? Well, you could learn, and quite possibly you could learn a lot, but I want to be emphatic about saying that you could not learn the same thing, even if you found classes with the same teachers. As an architect, I observed long ago that all of our senses respond to our environment, and I believe that learning is best accomplished when as many of the senses as possible are stimulated. This place, this sun-dappled, forested, flowered, fresh-aired place, and the people in it, provide for me that stimulation. I have also seen that we are more open to new ideas when we physically and mentally remove ourselves from the everyday demands and inputs of our lives. I'm hardly the first to extol the virtues of a retreat, nor is The Clearing the first to offer such an experience (though they've been at it for a very long time); it is simply one of the best.

Of course, you could come here and just relax. Great place for it. Meditate on limestone bluffs sitting in the shade of ancient wind-shaped cedars, overlook shimmering water. Groove on sunsets and good company. Imagine the founder of this place sitting in the chair you now occupy You need to do that. But I find myself working harder here than anywhere else, just because I want to. To show those around me what I can do, but far more importantly, to show myself. I can only speak as a writing student, but I suspect the photographers and philosophers, the woodworkers and weavers who come here have the same experience.

Norbert Blei did take me under his wing, and beneath that generous span I found a covey of other writers in all stages of their individual journeys, many already with an impressive list of publications to their credit, but some just starting out, as I was. And here's the thing I hadn't counted on, or even thought about, really: This group was to become home-base for me. These people are as varied in background and interests as I can imagine, but all hold dear the learning experience we have shared and the friendship we continue to share. All hold dear the individual and group help so lavishly heaped upon us by our leader, our teacher, our friend, Norb Blei; but then too, we are mightily enriched by the honest criticisms as well as the praises from each other. We revel in each other's victories and commiserate when our outcomes are something less than victorious. The Clearing is our center-point, and each year some of us are able to attend and some aren't, but there is always communication, there is always sharing. As a writer in the very earliest stages of my development, I could not imagine a better opportunity. Now, as a writer who fancies himself at an intermediate level, I feel quite sure that for me, a better learning situation simply doesn't exist.

I return to The Clearing, bodily, whenever I can. I return, in spirit, whenever I need.

Jude Genereaux

Clearing the Way

Ardent Peninsula Park campers, on a rainy day in August 1985 or 6 or 7, our family trooped through the pottery dens and gift shops of northern Door to amuse ourselves and get dry. A watercolor of a gull perched on a pier caught my eye and I picked up a copy of *Door Way*, thumbed through the pages to find "Dar, Woman Alone." After a moment scanning, I knew I wanted to know more about Dar, bought the book and squirreled it away in my backpack.

Not only did the story of Dar catch my interest, but in another chapter, author Norbert Blei wrote of a folk school on the isle of Door I was not aware of – "The Clearing." A place of rustic authenticity where he held a writing class each June. With summer camp etched deep in my being, the vision he created called me to know more about this place, and the following summer, my husband and I boldly drove in the grounds, following the curving road quietly through a meadow to find the quaint stone cottages hidden deep inside. More than a little unnerved, I expected at any moment the likes of a park ranger would jump out and demand we leave … just a little further on, we crept into a turn-about where I was able to glimpse just enough of the wooded walks and dark timbered buildings to kindle a yearning to be there.

But raising teens soon-to-be-college boys were years when dollars were tight, so my desire simmered on the back burners of priorities, fed by an almost annual search for this Writer's work. This man who talked of how it feels to be an immigrant after moving from Chicago to rural areas and feeling different; of being Czech and the heritage he treasured, of needing to write and get past the daily demands of all that keeps us from it. He was talking to me: a Czech, 'immigrated' from Motown to the northwest territory of Norwegian culture and agrarian life in Wisconsin.

1993. One son out of college and the second securely "in" brought some ease in finances. I wondered if Mr. Blei still taught the writing class noted in DOOR WAY, for he wrote that each year he debated his return. I wrote to him, asking, adding why I wanted to attend and why I felt connected to what he had to say. To my surprise, I received a handwritten note from him, encouraging my attendance, saying he would write again after his

Clearing the Way

return from an art show (his) in Santa Fe. But other events took precedence again that year ... but in the winter of '94, another letter left Rice Lake for Ellison Bay, this time netting a 5-page response. I was hooked.

June 11, 1994. After some last-minute doubts stemming from events that nearly crowded out my desire to attend, I headed across state as late as possible that Sunday, still dressed in sloppy boating gear and not as focused on the coming week as I was on Lake Superior in my rear view mirror. I knew the way to Ellison Bay as well as my own town after 20 years camping in Door, but the road into the Clearing was marked only by a low key black, wrought iron sign easily overlooked. This lent a mystical quality to finding the entry rather similar to that which Harry Potter must have felt seeking "Platform 9-3/4" at the train station on his journey to his school of wizardry and enchantment. After passing and returning to the winding road, I then had to guess my way to the Lodge, find someone who knew where I was to be, and then get there: in the '90s there was far less formal direction and signage, paperwork & maps directing our moves, so that first day retained a quality of discovery even as we merely searched for dinner.

Dinner. A hum of conversation floated from the open windows of the rock & timber solid Lodge filled with Frank Lloyd Wright style furnishings, shelves lined with books and a cathedral window framing the great Lake of Michigan that surrounds Door. Someone was playing a selection from "St Elmos Fire" on the small baby grand piano within and I felt a nearly audible 'click' inside of me as I let go the rush of the long drive, pushing out the many buzzing bees of a mind distracted by Too Much. I remember entering, standing back from the 25 or so writers waiting for the final dinner bell to gong, watching their interaction, feeling peaceful. I took a random place at the middle table, still dressed in boating cut-offs and a French sailors tee, expecting the week to begin tomorrow.

I was wrong. The Week began – Now. The last student was seated. Our host, Don Bucholz was at the head of my table when a rustle went up behind me, causing me to turn my head. I was startled to see him, Norbert Blei, entered the side door to the room and quietly scooted into his chair at the table behind me. There, he was there, here, with all of us waiting to hear him, meet him, see him. I didn't expect he would be with us until class in the morning. The air felt charged, and for reasons I was yet to learn, his presence nearly always created this. When he announced that the "Beginners" would meet after dinner in the Professor's Quarters, I immediately regretted I'd not changed into more appropriate attire. And so it began.

I walked the wooded paths around the rustic buildings after that first gathering. At night a few foot lights led the way to the Schoolhouse, but the blackness of the Door sky studded with stars was overwhelming company. Voices could be heard moving down the stone walks to nearby buildings; often laughter and the piano sent lilting messages of calm, reflection and "something higher" to be found here. My one roommate and I shared a rustic cabin with room for three, so it was spacious yet cozy in the dark wood of the older Clearing buildings. She, in the Advanced class, was inclusive, engaged – and gone most of the time, sleeping in the Cliff House at night and riding bike between classes as she tumbled over thoughts on work she brought. She told me how Norbert had been able to see the theme in her scattered work, guiding her to bring it together in a collection of short stories. This was something I heard time after time from others: the genius of the man as Teacher was helping direct his students find their own voice.

I still have my notes & scribblings from that first week reminding me of assignments and attempts to write Haiku, poetry, short stories - what they were, who we should read – authors I knew nothing of – William Carlos William, Grace Paley … what we needed to do: "Remember your dreams" "Be your own teacher"; advice & direction: "Essays analyze, tell you … short stories SHOW you;" "Every time you start to write of an event – you end up moving backward as well as forward" … "Draw on your resources, not on your angst." And I learned how important a clean, well-lighted place can be.

As well as the brilliance of our master teacher, talented writers attending from all fields of work encouraged my feeble attempts to contribute, inspiration coming from all sides – these people were Writers. And I wanted to be one, as inadequate as I felt. All of us wanted time with Norb and waited in line after class, made appointments to go over our work, or caught him at the Council Ring for a quiet moment. He always made time, took our work seriously. Fellow students spent dedicated hours writing between sessions, sitting on benches found in the dark green glens of The Clearing or overlooking the vistas of blue water in the bay. Sunny afternoons were spent with notebooks & pen, writing in quiet solitude or in groups sharing work, critiquing, encouraging. Friendships were made in this passage that remain, years and miles between.

Last day: Friday arrived in a blast of blue skies and a rush of anticipation for the evening's program. We would read our work, our best attempts, to each other. Scant moments were left until it was ended – a week of reverie and retreat. The sense of "too soon" pervaded the room as we all gathered in the amber light of the Lodge. The Founder, Jens Jensen looked down on us from the wall, proud of what he had done. We listened to each other, sipping a glass of wine, gnoshing, laughing, going into and out of ourselves en group. No one wanted to leave. Ever. As I sat listening to our people – Edith, Jackie, Alice, Donna, Stilinovich, Marianne – read, I sensed a presence behind me: from one of the

Clearing the Way

mission oak chairs, the low resonance of his voice asked if, after the Reading, would I like to walk the path to the schoolhouse with him, one more time? A prickle of alarm, fear, anticipation and Yes rumbled through my core. If I tell you The Clearing and a book changed my life, it would only be the beginning of this story.

Sharon Auberle

The Hawk in My Heart

Until I met Norbert Blei, I did not know there was a hawk in my heart. I had suspected something with wings lived there, because I could feel the thrashing of feathers now and then. Even wrote a (bad) poem about it. I knew that it was my creativity that was imprisoned, needed release, but until I attended The Clearing and met Norbert Blei the bird remained, frustrated and frantic in my heart.

"...as false as choosing to write about the bluebird of happiness in your eye, rather than the hawk in your heart." ~ N. Blei

These words are heavily underlined in a journal I kept during one of my week-long workshops with Blei at The Clearing School in Ellison Bay. They are not from the first workshop I took with him so long ago—1988 to be exact. But they describe, perfectly, how my writing changed over the years I studied with him.

When the student is ready, the teacher will appear.

In the spring of 1988 I had no idea either that the student (me) was ready, or that the teacher (Blei) would appear. One gray, late winter day, I picked up the *Chicago Tribune* to find an article that captivated me. The photos depicted serene, wooded paths, a solitary figure walking among them. There were buildings—vine-covered, stone and wood, listed on the National Historic Register.

I pored over the words of Jens Jensen and Mertha Fulkerson, and learned of the folk-oriented school for the arts established by Jensen high on a bluff overlooking the waters of Green Bay. Determined to go there, though I'd done nothing like this in my life before, I was hooked.

A few weeks later I saw in a local newspaper that the man who'd written one of my favorite books—*Door Steps*—would be signing copies at Townhouse Books in St. Charles, IL. I met Norbert Blei that day, he signed my book, and convinced me to attend the place that would become one of the passions of my life. The student was ready, the teacher had appeared.

Like so many others who come to his writing classes, I'd written sporadically, talked about "becoming serious about writing" and never did. And the mere thought of standing in front of a group of people to read was simply unthinkable. I was a timid soul but in that small bookstore beside the Fox River I committed, with great trepidation, to taking his class. That night I recorded a dream in my journal. In it Blei picked me up and in one fell swoop, turned me upside down—laughing wildly all the while. Little did I know how accurate this metaphor would turn out to be!

So there I was a few months later, toting a manual typewriter; wannabe-writer's hat in hand, overwhelmed both by the beauty of place and the enormity of what I'd done—come here, knowing no one, exposing all the angst and anxiety of my writing dreams to this group of strangers.

There was Emma, a grand lady with a passion and knowledge of birds and flowers unmatched by anyone I'd ever known. Ageless Edith, who must have been in her seventies then (she lived well into her nineties, still attending Norbert's classes) speaking of black lovers and her neighbors—the Hemingways; there was the clan of older ladies wandering the woods at night pursuing Indian spirits; Donna, who tossed the I-Ching each morning in the courtyard: Thea, of the many colorful scarves draped over her dorm bed; and Idessa, the self-described, crazy shopaholic. This was a radically different group of people than I'd ever met before...

Each day, when I wasn't wandering, enthralled, along the many paths of the Clearing, I would sit in class, listening to Norbert, doodling the same thing over and over—the tall schoolhouse windows, as if I needed to let light into my mind, clear out the old, dusty cobwebs of neglect. There was much lively conversation, and I took copious notes, but rarely opened my mouth, overwhelmed and outclassed as I felt.

Finally, one day, from out of nowhere my mind had ever gone before, a poem appeared. And I was amazed—I liked it, the teacher liked it, the class liked it!

NIGHT AT TAOS

blow, purple wind
ride your wild horse tonight
my sundown man comes
enfolds me in his blanket.
with turquoise, coral and jet
we paint our medicine in the sand
and your icy fingers
will not reach in here this night

The rest is history, but I remember one thing quite clearly—an evening excursion during that week to the AC Tap. In the tavern that night, I looked at myself in the washroom mirror and did not recognize the woman looking back at me. She was new, confident and secure in her dreams. A journal entry after I returned home says it all:

I have just finished the most creative, mystical, spiritual, productive and sensual week of my life. The woman that went to the Clearing is gone. The new woman is on her way...

These days "that thing with feathers that perches in my soul" as Emily Dickinson describes it, is no longer a shy bluebird. It is a hawk—fierce and wild, flying free.

Jackie Langetieg

Meeting Myself at The Clearing

It was a long Wisconsin drive, from Monona to Ellison Bay. I wondered if it would be worth it, this week in the woods, this escape from my life. It was 1986 and my marriage was pretty much ashes. I didn't know it then, but the next five years would require the respite of a week at The Clearing to help me get through them.

I threaded my way through the peninsula towns: Institute, Egg Harbor, Fish Creek, Ephraim, Sister Bay. Each little town was quaint, as I progressed from inland Door to the tourist meccas along highway 42. In Ellison Bay I turned left at Gus Klenke's Garage, a deserted building, grass grown around the door, a faded red sign naming this landmark. A little farther and I saw the sign for The Clearing and left turn; I almost missed it because it was the same color as the trees around it.

Driving through the coolness, I let out a breath I didn't know I'd been holding. This was lovely; if nothing else, this week, I would have this road to walk. I'd originally looked for music instruction, but settled for a week of writing——something, I hoped, would find its way to paper, but the further I drove into this place, the more I knew it wouldn't matter.

My roommate was already there, a woman from Chicago named ClaraMay. From her voice, I knew she was a smoker and, like me, a recovering alcoholic, so it seemed fate that we had been paired as roommates. She was in the Advanced Class, I was a Beginner, and we would have slightly different schedules. We hit it off right away and spent the first night talking until midnight.

My writing experience consisted of transcribing government rhetoric from a dictaphone into letters and mimeographs and very little else. I had a reputation for doing schtick from the "rules" that were passed down from the Administrative Office and had a group of people who followed my satires. I had written a newsletter when I was eight or nine, using a dial-a-letter, kiddy press typewriter. During my drinking years, I'd written bad poetry, including frustrated pencil stabs into the paper. That was the sum total of my writing experience. Somehow I knew that this place would change my life.

The highlight of the week was Norb. I was eager to learn and with his suggestions and prompts, I wrote both prose and poetry. This first week at The Clearing was the

Meeting Myself at The Clearing

beginning of almost thirty years of putting words down on paper giving me more pleasure than anything I'd done before, with writing, painting or music. We all wanted to be great for Norb – the women got crushes on him and he seemed to bond with the few men in the group.

In the beginners' group, one of the assignments was to write an essay about The Clearing. We had all week to do this, Friday looming large as the days went by. I was using a portable typewriter and when I finished my project, I gave a sigh of relief and a "Yeah" and slammed the top down on the portable case, cutting the electric chord and blowing the fuses for at least three cabins. The graciousness of Don Bucholtz saved me from dying of embarrassment. The next twenty-five years brought new friends, increased love of poetry, some facility in writing and a week to look forward to all year long.

The benefits were many: the lasting friendships, brilliant poppies, bells that call us to meals, Cliff House, the fire circle, Friday night parties, and the glorious sunsets. The weather has been as changeable as weather is in Wisconsin. One year it was so hot, the black top was melting and sticky. There were no fans in the cabins, and the stores in these little towns hadn't much to offer in the way of fan inventory, so I felt I was melting too. Many years have been filled with rain and thunder boomers, some cold enough for extra blankets but, without fail, the sun comes out part of the time to give us the opportunity to have a drink and share some chips and crackers before supper. The second year I went, there was a young woman with a flute and the sound of her playing added another dimension to the peace of the setting. Each year I returned to greet more friends until the week resembled a reunion as much as a learning experience.

As the years progressed, I learned about writers from many countries and ethnicities. One year I was Norb's "helper" and checked assignments and was in charge of one class of poetry for the beginners. There have been many helpers over the years, culminating the past five or so with Susan O'Leary shouldering the responsibility of the beginning class. Susan is a Buddhist and has shared the experience of walking meditation and her calm demeanor and sense of humor. Two others that made a lasting impression were Edith Nash and Joe Patrick, both gone now.

In January, 2003, my son died. The months following were difficult. I drove into The Clearing's shaded lane and cried all the way to the parking lot. A dear friend had lost her son two weeks after mine, and we shared a room that year and gave each other strength. I began to write the book about Jason that would eventually become *Just What Is A Stage Of Grief*. Each poppy seemed to bloom for me that summer.

Jackie Langetieg

I originally thought I'd miss the music, but music goes on independently. People bring their instruments, I've carried a guitar back and forth a few times. For a number of years the Peninsula Music Group always gave their concert at the Schoolhouse, filling the air with lovely ensemble orchestra and groups of strings and piano solos. This past year, our dear friend Aldo brought a Native American flute, and haunting notes filled the room along with his beautiful poetry. The Clearing has been and continues to be my entertainment, education, solace and haven and where I have found my better self as each year passes.

> "Writing is a long journey toward an authentic self and setting."

Writing is a long journey toward an authentic self and setting.
Norbert Blei, from "North of Kafka," Winter Book

On your journey towards authenticity, what do you need?

Certainly not answers, for this is your journey after all. You must find your own way. But the right questions from a friend (the friend part is essential) and road maps showing what route others have taken–not that you will do the same–help as you set out on this adventure. It's good to begin from a special place as well, a place on the edge, where the difference between getting away from it all and getting closer to authenticity can happen.

The Clearing in Door County was such a place; the friend was Norb Blei. When I arrived there for my first workshop with Norb Blei, I felt this edge, and though I had been writing before I came, it seemed that there was much more for me to discover. As I drove into the Clearing, it was as if I were driving into deep mystery. The tree-covered road that twists and turns, that brings you into a wide open clearing where you see the sky, and then sends you down the rest of the drive under spreading branches–this could have been a metaphor for the journey I was about to undertake.

I arrived. I parked. I followed a path. My room was homey, like visiting my grandmother, and I felt that it had been prepared just for me, only for me. The soft handmade quilt on the bed, beautiful wooden furniture, floors, and walls, my room was tidy and efficient, giving me everything I needed.

Norb's presence was immense. Each time I met him, I felt this presence, this Czech-American with a walrus-like mustache, barrel chest, deep, booming voice. I trembled, pushed towards him "my work," afraid to hear what he'd say. No judgments were passed, much to my relief. Instead he asked questions, listened, paused, looking off into some distant place. He threw out a few ideas, and I scribbled notes to myself, hoping I would be able to catch their meaning later.

Then class. He didn't lecture. He passed out page after page of writing. Photocopies of a favorite poem, a short story, a page from a book. Not his. No, I would have to find that on my own. Other writers. He read voraciously. Following his reading paths, I could never keep up. He read from these sheets aloud, in that deep rich timbre. And then we discussed. And so it went. By now, the Clearing had become my world. There was no other world, just this one, where words matter. I followed the gentle path back to my cabin, or down to the lake, discovering a cairn left for contemplation; or through the woods, visiting some feature of The Clearing's landscape designed by Jens Jensen, the Council ring, or dance ring, or Cliff House, all the while mulling over everything I'd taken in. There were always other students like me to laugh with, eat with, get to know, but at the end of the day, as I lay in bed waiting for sleep, I felt the question rising again: what is my truth?

Norb didn't want to be called teacher, or mentor. He autographed his books using "in friendship." He never said if what was written was good or bad. I brought words to him, and he read them, and responded from his vast knowledge of literature, but never judgment of worth. Read this, he'd say, thrusting a book my way, or tell me to look up so and so when I was home again. So unlike previous methods of learning. Frightening stuff to the unsure, but the only way, in Norb's view of teaching. The student teaches him or herself, not the teacher. Find your own answers.

As time passed, even though I was no longer at the Clearing, I stayed connected to Norb. He took time to write me many emails, letters, sent clippings, and books for me to read. His message always was, "I believe in you." So many depended on him for this kind of support, and he gave, and gave, and gave.

I am still on a path, finding my way, but going in a direction no one else is following in exactly the way I am. It often feels like a beginning, but the question: "is it good?" has seemed to disappear. The journey towards authenticity is what matters.

The Teacher

I came to The Clearing for the first time sixteen years ago, dreaming of being a writer; not just a writer, but a great one. I believed one could design a creative prose with simple words that miraculously attached to a reader's imagination; taking them on a journey of fantasy through their own interpretation of the story I was telling, just by using the technical writing skills I practiced daily. Then I met Norbert Blei.

Norb was kind to beginning creative writers, giving them leading lines to write against, to develop their skill of short story or poetry. He was patient with people like me who presented with technical writing skills, teaching us how to break through the formal directive or prescriptive style of writing; to allow our thoughts to flow freely, and drop to the page with each touch of the pen. Perhaps not always making sense at first, but with re-working, able to involve the reader in the storyline. Norb taught me to "unzip" myself from the professional setting and free my imagination; to tell my stories with creative dialogue, description, and enough information to engage the reader.

Over the years, I came to think of Norb as "the master of writing" who demonstrated his talent for linking words that floated on the page, inviting a reader to join him in neighborhoods, on streets, and in places that came to life with all the scents, sounds, and characters that were a part of the story. I wanted to write like that, but he taught me I had my own stories to tell through my own words, while giving me the understanding and knowledge I needed.

I came to The Clearing writing simple words that fell flat on paper. I am still a writer of simple words but now I understand the true art of writing. I met a professional but kind man who shared his wisdom with a beginning writer from the first day we met at The Clearing. I no longer dream of writing a great novel to be put on a shelf, but to write for the benefit of writing. My words still fall flat, but through rework… and rework…and rework, I can create a rhythm and flow of thought that is creative.

Norb used the backdrop of natural beauty of The Clearing and Door County in his own writing and books. He gave to me not only words of wisdom, but demonstrated a respect for the beauty of God's gifts in landscapes, nature, waterways, and the people of Door County. He once told me I was a pioneer woman. To this day I am not sure what he meant, but for me he was the pioneer. He knew genre, but had his own stories to tell in his own way, through writing, art, and photography. He helped me to understand that my simple way of writing is my own way of storytelling, and that is okay.

    Norb, Thank you for the lessons learned, for your patience, and for becoming my friend.

Finding The Way Home

I've known only two Norberts in my life: my father, Norbert Beauchamp, who transitioned to the next dimensional plane on the 1st of January 1989, and Norbert Blei, who joined him on the 23 of April 2013.

The importance for me in this unlikely pairing is that my father was a seafaring man, with the salt and wind in his veins, and Norb was a man of the earth, fire, and seasons. I love the blend of the elemental qualities of these men. They both shared the same first name, and both wrote poetry, which is what ultimately inspired me to come to the Clearing seven years ago.

A now lost-to-me friend knew I was looking for a writer's retreat; a place to nestle in with nature and the elements, to write with other writers, to spend quiet time with the nature of me related to the nature of a forest, a lake, a meadow, birds, and the likelihood of annoying insects. I wanted a place where a writer could feel the inspiration of the wind, rain, sun, all the quietude and noise of the flora and fauna. She asked had I ever heard of this place called The Clearing, a folk arts school in Door County, WI? She said it was all those things I imagined having. That's what she said. In that moment I believed her. That was a cold February day seven years ago. I Googled it when I got home.

The Clearing website was well laid out and lovely, the photos stunning. I was captured and pulled in immediately by the visuals. All the luscious green, and those tall Sister pines, the miles of white lake rock, the log buildings, the precarious retreat at the edge of a cliff overlooking Green Bay, I thought, 'Good Lord what was that?' There was a maze of narrow paths that zigged and zagged through lush woods, connecting the main lodge with the housing and workshop buildings and leading to Circles, to workshops, to more paths, and to the Lake. I could imagine the waft of the fresh green and pine with the wildness of the trillium scattered in the woods... All that glorious trillium!

North of the lodge, the housing, and workshop buildings stood The Jensen Center with its oddly modern look of wood and stone comfortably set into the natural surrounds. Inside, were books, and art, literature about the surrounding area, other places to visit, galleries to see and a Great Room for teaching and other events. There were windows that let in perfect light, and what seemed like endless woods and blue sky. I wanted to go there.

I clicked on the brochure page of classes and information. I was breathing fast and heavy by this point. My eyes were ready to look for the writing possibilities. With one

Jeanne Adwani

click, there was Norbert Blei, with his white shag of hair, that big mustache, his rather stern and rugged look. So earthy. Such a different kind of Norbert to the slick, bohemian style of my father with his beret tilted at the perfect rakish angle, and his ever-present smile.

I locked in. Norb's class description gave a detailed synopsis of the week-long poetry writing class he was teaching to "the advanced" student, with his associate, Susan O'Leary teaching 'beginners'. His offerings were intimidating and overwhelming. Definitely advanced beyond my comfort zone. I didn't feel like a beginner either. Other offerings for the week allowed me to come as an "independent" and hang out, write without any expectation; make it more of a solitary retreat, joining the group for meals and conversation. Though I was intimidated, I decided I didn't care. I was hungry for a piece of this offering. It resonated in my heart, pulling me right down to the land and the smell of green and those cool white stones that blanketed the beach.

I never got to read any of my father's poems. I was denied them by a bitter woman. I had my fantasies of what they might hold, of what the sea and the foreign places that took him away for months at a time might have felt like. What might the incredible potential for solitude on a huge ocean vessel be? What loneliness might he have felt? What was it about the vast expanse of the sea and nowhere even a slip of land? What pulled my father into this kind of life? How might he write of that vastness, his loneliness?

My Norbert of sea and wind, had called me to this Norbert of earth and fire, along the cliffs and fresh air of Green Bay. I knew without a pause that I was to join this group. I was to go to the Clearing and be with Norbert Blei and Susan O'Leary. I knew without a doubt that the vast sea breeze of me was going to have a forest of green and plenty to look out from and come back to, to write in. I called immediately, and signed up.

My Norberts are gone now. I really don't care if I meet another. What I care about is that I get to go back to the Clearing every year and be on the land, smell the lake, and forest, walk the Labyrinth, ponder what I have learned from my teachers here. Dream in quietude of the nights teased with the song of the cicada. Listen with deep intent to what the land has to say to me, so that I can find the words that rise up from my sensory experiences, and lay them down.

Birthed from salt and sea
His forest words a labyrinth
Clearing the way home

Clarity & Calm

"If you're interested in writing, you should attend Norb Blei's workshop at The Clearing," said an artist friend, Win Jones. He described a folk school in northern Door County with log cabins and a school house along Lake Michigan shores. "You don't cook or do chores. You commune with nature. Everything you need is provided by the staff. Norb and I have been conducting workshops there for thirty years."

The Clearing. Perhaps a good place for me to sort out what I am meant to do.

I'd struggled for several years after back-to-back losses: my ninety year old mother, followed by my seventy-five year old cousin, Sister Saint Jean. My cousin's passing was particularly heartbreaking. We lived near each other. Twenty five years older than me, she provided significant emotional support while I broke free of an abusive marriage, earned a college degree and created a healthier life for my three children. I became one of my cousin's care-givers during her rugged battle with lung cancer. She continued to counsel me. "Always seek the calm. You'll find it when you are doing what you were meant to do."

After these deaths I returned to work. It didn't fill my emptiness. I sought refuge in the arts. I took piano and voice lessons, and attended classes at a local college in drawing, ceramics and writing. Time and the arts lifted me out of my depression. Music stirred my feet to dance and caused my fingers to play on imaginary keys. Rekindled emotions compelled me to write when I woke up and at every opportunity during the day. I penned images and feelings until my fingers cramped, my back ached, and my vision blurred.

I considered The Clearing.

I vacillated. *I have too many responsibilities here.*

I capitulated. *No harm in checking it out.*

I called and was accepted as an Intermediate Writer.

The workshop description included notes from Norb, "This year's seminar for advanced writers will focus on *The Writing Life*."

Perfect, I thought. *Just what I need* and continued reading Norb's words.

"...We have all read more than enough books on how to write. Useless! Our focus...will deal instead with how we live or fail to live our life, and what we make of it – in writing."

Required reading included books by Orwell, Virginia Woolf, Annie Dillard, Duras, Saroyan, and M.F.K. Fisher, followed by a long list of suggested readings.

I moaned. "What have I gotten myself into?"

Catherine Hovis

Sunday, June 8, 2003, a few weeks before my fifty-seventh birthday, I drove north from Illinois plains to Wisconsin hills. When I arrived at The Clearing I wound through dense woods and past a field of indigenous grasses. I parked my car under a canopy of trees. Verdant smells of rupturing spring with grass, trees, and moist ground, assailed me. I walked toward a collection of weathered log cabins. Sorta like summer camp, I thought, while I continued past them to a main lodge. A woman with a big smile greeted me and reviewed a map of the grounds. I gathered my Clearing information to join the writers who filled all the cabins and headed out to meet my roommate in cottage #8.

It had been a long time since I'd shared space with a stranger so I was a little hesitant about the arrangement. Alice D'Alessio, tall, slim, with a ready smile below short dark hair, greeted me. She settled me into our room equipped with a pair of twin beds topped with hand-made quilts; a far cry from summer camp. We had desks, a built in cupboard for our clothes, and our own bathroom.

Alice said she was an early to bed, early to rise person. I'm a late to bed, early to rise person, yet, that night, I was the first one to turn off my light.

At 5:30 the next morning I wrote, "I'm having difficulty transitioning into being here…phone calls I should have made…welfare of everyone back home. I'm intent on feeling guilty…"

Alice, a long-time attendee, prose and poetry writer, shepherded me through the routine of bells calling us to three meals a day and the daily schedule of the writing workshop sessions; beginners first, advanced last.

My overachiever genes kicked in. I committed to attending all of the classes, in addition to going on walks, outings, and to nightly campfires.

On Tuesday, I wrote in my journal, "…talented writers here…unlimited riches within their minds…humble in this group…their drive to write rubbing off on me. Here I nurture my spirit. …I want to work on my words, release my voice, test it in this remarkable place, The Clearing…"

I became exhausted but I couldn't stay away from any of the sessions. Norb's assistant, Susan O'Leary, slender, quiet, with knowing eyes, introduced a writing form I hadn't encountered. The ancient art of haiku, a minimalist story form – a three line verse of five, seven, then five syllables. Her writing methods challenged me to find the exact words. I couldn't resist accompanying Susan the day she led a merry band of writers through the woods. She pointed out the poetry in the surroundings and spoke of healing in its peace; the same observations my cousin Sister Saint Jean would have made.

Norb Blei was bigger than life, beyond my expectations. An impassioned prolific writer, with a thick handle-bar mustache, graying wiry hair, and bushy brows, he commanded our attention. "There is never enough time, never enough days for the reading and writing you must do." He fed us, "Oh, and then there's this," and on the last day his book bag was stuffed to overflowing with copies of stories and numerous books he still needed to share with us. He had to open our minds to every possible writing avenue. It was as if he proclaimed, "There's gold in them thar hills. Read and read, and write and write, and read and write some more, and you will discover it."

In the exodus from worldly demands, I relaxed. I allowed The Clearing to work its magic through the ministrations of staff, teachers, and developing friendships. Among them, Edith Nash, with her coiffed white curls, who always sat to Norb's left during the advanced class; his protégé in spite of her senior years.

I talked with Edith in the main lodge. She sat in a rocking chair in front of a tall window which offered a view of lush bushes and evergreens against a backdrop of blue sky and water. Edith listened while I mulled over if I was meant to be a writer. And, if so, how could I possibly alter my life to venture onto a new path?

"You can do it, if it's important enough," she said with quiet resolve and a firm nod of her head. "If it's important, you will do it."

Within the security of The Clearing, I gave voice to suppressed emotions. I stunned myself by reading my poem, "Papa's Entrance," to a room full of accomplished writers. I closed with the last line, "Papa dined on booze, danced on joy, and stole the laughter from my soul."

I wrote, "Writing is taking hold – be clear, be succinct – story…isn't an 18 page formula, it can be as little as a paragraph… Peace and urgency are at war. I'm looking closer for the calm within the path of my words."

On a story I'd given to Norb, he wrote, "Great sense of narrative. But, this is a short story that got away." He revealed what worked, then gave me something more to strive for.

Susan's notes to me at the end of the week referenced two of my assignments, "Tight structure & excellent last line in the poem. Clear writing & content… You've made a big shift in your writing."

Before I left The Clearing, Norb asked about my goals.

I said, "I want to be a writer."

My honesty surprised me. I hadn't said *it's impossible, but I want to be a writer*. I hadn't said *I have so many responsibilities: business, community volunteer, wife, mother and grandmother. Another passion could not possibly fit into my life*.

He said. "*You are a writer.*"

I was restless during my drive back home, antsy to find a way to discuss my feelings with my husband and my oldest daughter. Their business lives would be impacted the most if I pursued a new direction as they would have to take over my responsibilities at our family business.

Always my most exuberant supporter, my husband said, "Yes, go for it."

My loving daughter said, "Yes, Mom, you deserve to pursue your goals."

With their support I developed a plan. To facilitate my change, I entered a master's program in creative writing. School became the upper authority. When someone called and asked me to become involved in their cause, I replied. "At any other time I'd be glad to help, but I'm going to school now." I became a community recluse, and allotted my precious spare time to my family and a few friends.

Ten years have passed since my first journey to The Clearing. And still it calls me for renewal. An entrenched member of the Blei Clan, I have returned at least once a year. Now, Norb's spirit demands that I press on. For him there was never enough time, never enough days to do it all. He bequeathed his urgency to each of his writers.

Norb was right; there will never be enough days. I must embrace the calm and write.

DyAnne Korda

The Perfect Gardener

On the afternoon of the Long Night's Moon, I wrote at my desk after a wintry walk with our husky. She and I stopped often so she could bury her face and dig in powdered snow, hunting for tiny critters skittering beneath steep drifts. Every turn of the trail, she pointed her nose high in grey skies, smelling the animal smells that accompany sharp, chilling winds. With every sniff, her eyes reflected calculations of the when, what, and who—somewhere out of sight.

Scott and I moved to northern Minnesota at the edge of wilderness because of our deep appreciation of the natural world like this one. Our writing sessions with Norbert Blei at the Clearing nourished that. And even though Norb's classes were usually in June, he asked his students to stop, reflect and become mindful, a practice that often happens now, at year's end.

The Clearing supplied the pure gift of natural settings for contemplation in order to rest, renew and begin again.ABjens Jensen, the founder, understood that coreopsis fields, limestone bluffs, birch with singing birds, turquoise bays, trillium, and forest floors are our original teachers. Perhaps he intuited that society would come close to dismissing the natural world before we realized the potential loss of its lessons. From my visits to the Clearing, here's something I easily picked up and have taken to heart: If we unplug from the hyper-twitter mania, we may get some fine guidance from the silence around us.

The Student

Student, what are you looking for along my shore, the Lake asks.
Reassurance, I whisper, swaying with the weight of rolling blue-gold water.

One eagle rises and rides spiraling breezes.
He seems willing to take my unprepared prayers
across Her drumming waves. His wings drift
through these words while Coyote naps, hidden among cedar.

Here and now, the Lake sings, *let me rinse your face and wash your feet while the wind tugs your clothing. Stay here*, She sings louder, *the dance is free and this is how I change the weather.*

The Perfect Gardner

At the beginning of each Clearing week, Norbert played the perfect gardener by quickly and casually assessing the class, then planting the necessary creative seeds. He not only considered the whole group's needs and interests, but those of the individuals within it. He cultivated and pruned our writing paths, giving his all. In turn, Norb expected us to plant ourselves in unfamiliar philosophies, send down a few discovery roots, and then take the chance to flourish. If we didn't learn something new about ourselves by week's end, what the hell was the point?

Norbert's thoughtful and well-researched presentations fired our imaginations. Each session usually had a particular theme, based within his immense range of interests. Students who regularly attended Norb's annual classes journeyed from Surrealism to Zen and beyond. We learned the basics of excellent poems and studied the intricacies of solid short stories. We were introduced to a wide watercolor palette of writers, artists and doers. *Edward Abby, Emma Toft, N. Scott Momaday, Georgia O'Keefe, Louise Erdrich, Gabriel Garcia Marquez, MC Richards, Frida Kahlo, Isabelle Allende.* They came with great imaginations from many cultures, breaking down complex ideas and illuminating wonders within simplicity. We realized a wealth of obstacles and joys—next door and worldwide. Sometimes we folded their influences into our own writing missions. *Kenneth Patchen, Francis May, Bill Stipe, Naomi Shihab Nye, Lao-Tsu, Dave Etter, Gary Snyder, Charles Simic, Maya Angelou, Sandra Cisneros, Thich Nhat Hanh.*

Norbert chose to nurture serious writing students and allowed wannabes to weed themselves out before his next year's class. He had little patience for those who noodle around and only *talk* about *wanting* to begin that best-selling novel. He understood those of us who write madly because we simply can't help it. We pay attention to details, find the exact word and get it down.

And it's good to be among fellow writers around the dining table. The Clearing gave us gifts of small community with food, drink and time. Time to truly listen and consider one another's stories. As Barry Lopez said, "If stories come to you, care for them. And learn to give them away where they are needed. Sometimes a person needs a story more than food to stay alive."

We learned that to be writers, slowing down and paying attention with open eyes and heart is necessary. When life spins out of control, I remind myself that the Clearing's routine brings me back in balance: the arts, reading and, like this afternoon, walking in nature with our dog. These acts allow me to relocate my spirit and feed it. They bring me back to my desk with a fast pen in hand on ice-blue afternoons surrounding the Long Night's Moon.

Scott and I enjoy imagining the Clearing during the deepest cold and silent months. During this dark winter season of gratitude, I offer thanks for all the Clearing has provided—for giving Norbert Blei a place in the presence of woods, wildflowers and water to inspire writers, then send us on our way.

Scott Stowell

Beyond Postcards

Snow squeaks under my footsteps like high-end cheese curds on teeth. The thermometer reads 33-below zero at five o'clock on Christmas Eve morning. I walk to my truck in the dark, unplug the engine block heater and hook the stiff power cord on the wall inside the garage. The cord never really gives up its loop from having spent the night outdoors. This is bound to happen in the Minnesota Arrowhead 12 miles from the Canadian border. But I've got a job to do on a morning when most of my co-workers have the whole day off. Even before starting the truck, I say to myself, "I can live with this." I turn the key and the engine fires.

I blame The Clearing for these pleasures.

The Clearing is a harbor for working on dreams. Along with a clearing in the woods and a clearing of time, it is a cleared space in my head. It allowed me to nurture passions and immerse myself in other realms, especially imagination. Even its exquisite architecture and landscape invite spirited exploration.

The Clearing casts a medieval appearance that reminds me of *Monty Python and the Holy Grail*. So liberated were my wife DyAnne and I upon our first-ever arrival, that we wheeled our bags into our cabin with one of the handy garden carts, then reenacted the "Bring out Your Dead" scene from the Python film. I plopped her inside the cart and we made our way from building to building and tree to tree admiring the grounds.

Early in a Clearing week, I'd glom space inside the Schoolhouse with alpha ferocity. I staked my personal writing camp by the cathedral window overlooking Lake Michigan and concocted a daily ritual of hot Friendship Tea from the Schoolhouse kitchenette. Don't get me wrong. I'm not one to shirk the delights of well-timed gin or summertime suds. And within my normal state of mind, the phrase "friendship tea" connotes a kind of Kumbaya, Lawrence Welkian experience. But this was The Clearing— and I set aside such perspective. I couldn't get enough of the stuff.

Norbert Blei, Coyote, was our mentor at The Clearing. His love of language and the power of words led him to freelance writing, journalism and publishing. Earlier in his career, he taught English in public schools, but left and became a teacher of a different sort. There was nothing namby-pamby about the guy, and his teaching methods sent us places.

One of the places we didn't go was grad school. Not that we're post-college snobs or the opportunity wasn't there. Many of our closest and respected friends have graduate

Beyond Postcards

degrees. But everyone learns and contributes in different ways, and after a while we opted out.

During my final trip to The Clearing, Norb invited a DJ from the local radio station to record interviews with the writing class about our works-in-progress. Radio is my favorite media. More than any of the others, radio is a constant companion throughout the year either upfront or in the background. It offers music, news, weather, ballgames, holiday specials and idle chitchat that often become memories of where I was when I first heard them. So when the radio guy arrived, I thought how gratifying it would be for the words we all spoke that night to eventually enter the homes, workplaces and car radios of willing listeners.

Later that summer, I left my career as an English teacher to actually do more of what I was trying to teach. I found work in radio as a copywriter.

Long story short, radio writing eventually led to a stint as a magazine editor until I was downsized. About that same time, DyAnne's primary employer passed away and we were both looking for work. It was one of those life-altering periods.

Thanks to Norb, I developed a personal take on writing fiction. It's basic but requires some effort: "Pay attention to life and put your imagination to the rest of it." So considering our employment situation, we set out to do some paying of attention. Hell, we could be unemployed anywhere. We took a leap on February 29th, a Leap Year Day, and moved to northern Minnesota. I found a job bartending and DyAnne got retail work selling mukluks.

The lifestyle isn't for everyone and some seasonal visitors might see it as a step down even though they secretly envy us for living here, a tourist sentiment not uncommon around Door County and The Clearing.

One day at the bar I waited on a pleasant couple who was on vacation to experience the natural beauty of the surrounding wilderness. They were the only ones in the place so I had extra time to talk to them. When they found I was once a magazine editor, the woman politely inquired how I felt now about being a bartender.

I hope I reciprocated with words to match her friendly demeanor because somewhere in my memory Norb was knocking at the door.

DyAnne and I purposely moved to a landscape that offers physical and spiritual grandeur. But, like The Clearing, the scenery goes far beyond a majestic backdrop of picture postcards and home décor publications. The postcards live. That big picture includes smelling cedar, touching greenstone, gazing over lakes, hearing wolves and—if I'm respectful—tasting venison.

There's also a full view of reality in the employment climate. Year-round residents take on an assortment of jobs to get by. So I told the couple I try not to get caught up in titles. There are many people in our town with advanced college degrees who are working in fields entirely unrelated to their formal education. Then I said, "Look where I get to live."

A few years later, I got lucky again and became the editor of one of our local newspapers. Trouble is, I hate journalism. But Norb stayed in touch and helped me understand the work. I ventured into another writing style, it entrenched me in the community and I got to help its characters tell their stories. They're much like the folks Norb wrote about who live near The Clearing.

Our local radio station has special programming on Christmas Eve and Christmas Day. That's where I'm headed. I work there now. I'm blessed with being on the microphone side of the morning show. If people are of a mind to tune us in, my broadcast partner and I are invited to play music and share stories that will be part of listeners' preparations for a very special day. Hopefully we'll add to their entertainment and maybe they'll remember moments that will stick as holiday memories or become a pleasant tradition in their household.

Deep cold on Christmas Eve morning. My truck starts. I still love radio. And I turn over pleasant thoughts of The Clearing. I can live with that.

Real Writers

Norb sat at the head of the table with books and copies of papers piled next to him, in front of him and behind him on the piano. His passion and reverence for literature was contagious. He was a lover of the words, stories and craft. We gathered at the schoolhouse for class, the tribe of writers glued to their favorite seats. Nature peeked into our sanctuary through the windows with no need of an invitation. Norb had the voice of a poet, he read to us from his favorite books. I was like a wide-eyed child, ravenous, thirsty and starving for the worlds he showed us, worlds that had escaped me. When Norb read out loud, the others disappeared from the long wood table. It was just two of us. He read me bedtime stories I had never heard. His stories tickled my heart. I could see and smell the details of smoky rooms and rocky riverbeds.

I had a secret among these accomplished writers. Reading evoked dread more than pleasure. I listened to the books Norb assigned us for class on tapes as I drove everywhere in my car. I feared I would never finish his assignments.

Norb taught us and showed us that writing was where we could tell our secrets. The page, he convinced us, was unafraid and could caress our pain and transform shame into a good story.

With our tummies satisfied from a Clearing-style three course breakfast, Norb invited us to read what we wrote the night before. That morning, I read my story and confessed the secret that haunted me.

Great writers are great readers. Rain is wet. Indisputable truths. I picture most writers sitting amidst books at every eye level: books covering the floor, on bookshelves, and the dining room table. They wrestle themselves to sleep at night, reluctant to put down their cherished novel, poetry or book of great essays. They wake in the morning and they may not brush their teeth before one of the three books they are reading appears in their hands. Reading, besides a source of constant pleasure, provides entry to worlds beyond daily reach. Words, phrases, meticulous details, metaphors, and the rhythm of the words dance on the page feeding the soul of the writer.

Then I remember Mrs. Jacobsen, my third grade teacher, reading the names for the Blue Bell Group: Lynn Marks, Louise VanBerg, Ann Fergueson. My friends from the basketball team. She continued. My name was not read. Next, the Sugar Plums:

Laurie Kahn

Randy Stoddard, Carolyn Worthington, Nancy Goddin, Dale Andrews. My friends from the kick ball game where we played shirts against no shirts on Kingston road. Still my name was not mentioned.

The name of the last group I believe was Dumb Bells, but I could be wrong. Patrinia Cann. Everyone knew Patrinia smelled bad and ate the erasers off her pencils and then swallowed them. Pete Wilkenson, a dwarf who on his tip toes came up to my waist. Then my name, Laurie Kahn. I remember that sick feeling inside when the world turned black, and from that day on nothing was ever the same.
I was in the lowest reading group.

School slowly moved from an annoyance to dread. I could not get this reading thing. The words didn't work for me. I looked at them the same way everyone else did, but they just didn't stick or mean anything to me. I wasn't trying to be difficult. Honestly, I would have done anything to get to a higher reading group and not have to sit next to Patrinia with her nasty bad breath and greasy hair.

I learned to get by. I absorbed everything the teacher would say. If we had tests based on reading rather than on what the teacher told us, I could sit next to Lynn Marks who would let me copy the answers off her paper.

In eighth grade my cover was blown. My parents hired a tutor named Mr. Harrison. On Wednesdays he would come to my house. We would sit at my mother's card table in the room with the bright green carpet. I would face the picture of a landscape with a boat by the water, wishing there was a way to transport myself to that land, wherever it might be and not sit at this table with Mr. Harrision. Mr. Harrison asked me to read out loud. I refused.

Eventually, I began looking forward to Mr. Harrison with his big belly coming to the house. He knew my secret and liked me. He told my parents I had dyslexia and he thought he could help me learn to read.

I read this to the class. My secret put on display, my heart was beating hard and fast, my hands trembled while my story vibrated in my hand as I read. I thought Norb would expel me from the class and find me a place for the seriously delayed writer. Instead, a smile relaxed into his white beard. His eyes spoke gentleness. He turned to me and said, "nicely written, Laurie."

Now I am a real writer. I have one book on my Kindle for when the lights are out, another dog-eared paperback with my comments scribbled in the margins, and another book that fits neatly in my purse for those unexpected moments when the noise stops and I can steal a few minutes to read. When I was forty I drove five hours to the Clearing. I attended Norb's class for six consecutive years. The Clearing is where I became a real writer. It is where I fell in love with the written word.

At fifty-five I received my MFA in Creative Non-Fiction. I am now wrestling with the last chapters of my own book.

Transformation

In 2001 I took a summer class at the Clearing. I'd taken winter classes for several years but this would be my first weeklong experience. I dove in and signed up for Norbert Blei's writing class. While I didn't exactly bellyflop during the week, I felt I was swimming out of my league.

Earlier I'd met Norb on paper as he'd graciously replied to letters I'd sent regarding his Cross+Roads Press and other matters. He had invited me to come on campus to hear a visiting author several summers before. But in the spring of 2001, I met Norb in person for the first time, on the sidewalk outside of Ace Hardware in Sister Bay. I identified myself and told him I was joining the class, and before I could thank him for his written replies he gave me a great big hug.

And so it was that in June I set foot on what I considered to be sacred grounds–where Jens Jensen had walked.

That first experience was emotionally charged for me. The branches along the path from the student parking lot draped over me and the breeze off the bay renewed my spirit. I could almost feel my body humming. Oh, I wanted to belong to this community of writers, but up until then my writing had consisted of letters and individual educational programs for special education students. As I approached the schoolhouse several people welcomed me. Edith Nash, whose sharp ear and helpful critiques I later came to appreciate, was one of them. While I remember few other specifics of that evening I remember feeling like a round peg in a round hole. These were people I wanted to get to know.

That summer week was one of total immersion. We read, we wrote, we talked, we laughed, we became community. I felt my chest loosen, my guard let down, my real self coming to life. My husband had died during the prolonged 2000 Presidential election. During this summer week I wrote my grief poem. Another woman had also recently lost her husband, and we shared sorrows, sadness, and silliness along with poetry in and out of class. I can truly say that the people I met that week, many of whom I still call "friend," eased my first widowhood journey. It became a journey into the light rather than a trip toward the dark side.

It's hard to separate the effect of the Clearing from the effect of Door County on one's psyche. Through both the winter and summer classes of the Clearing I have met the most amazing people, all educated, caring, generous, witty, and kind. One woman took me under her wing and helped me transform from a wallflower into an engaged listener and activist in a variety of activities. Several writers exposed me to the greater writing communities in the state and gave me fine writing to emulate. In addition they offered friendship, acceptance, and thoughtful advice. New skills emerged as a result of classes and the relationships I made. I think the gift of the Clearing is the people, and the gift of Door County is what remains of the unspoiled landscape.

In Norb's classes, and in classes with other writers, I'm struck by how quickly a "confidence of strangers" develops. A sense of trust travels through the instructor and within a day or two stories are opened, like long shoeboxed photographs, to be shared and examined. The compassion can be felt in the room as tissues wipe away tears, eyes meet, and long buried experiences are exhumed and demystified. Perhaps one can get this in therapy or at the neighborhood tavern, but at the Clearing that sharing leads each participant to a richer writing process.

I've taken other kinds of classes and a similar phenomenon happens. That "confidence of strangers" leads us away from daily routines and grants us the safety to examine our life and relationships. I'm sure that some individuals have returned home only to begin journeys they hadn't envisioned before their week at the Clearing.

It's been ten years since that first summer. I've had poems, prose, and press releases published. I've gained confidence in myself. I've joined writers groups and worked to initiate a Poet Laureate position in Door County. My life partner is a man I met at the Clearing. He is wonderfully kind and gentle and accepting of my foibles. After all, we met at the Clearing.

During all that time, I managed to always be on Norb's good side, as far as I know. He helped me to grow as a writer and I treasure the times we spent together at Al Johnson's, Base Camp, and at FishStock when it was still up in the loft. I fondly recall the evening Norb and Jude dined at my home near Moonlight Bay. We shared a love of artist books and, of course, small press offerings. There were always new literary discoveries to enjoy.

Coming Home to The Clearing

It was late October, 2003, and I was headed up to Wisconsin's Door County for the first time. I always like to research places I plan to travel to, and this time was no different. It took me a while to wade through all the websites filled with fish boils and cherry orchards, when, just days before I was to leave, I discovered The Clearing Folk School. Photographs of a stone lodge covered in ivy, log cabins, lush woodlands, and vistas opening to the vast expanses of Green Bay. This was my kind of place.

I saw that The Clearing offered weeklong classes, and the enticing list of art, nature, craft, and writing classes beckoned to me. I had been wanting to take a creative writing class of some kind, to shift from the professional and business writing that has always been a part of my job. I clicked on the link for "Writing Workshop" – and up popped a picture of the instructor, Norbert Blei. "Oh, so that's where he went to!" I thought to myself.

Blei and I had crossed paths before, only he didn't know it. When I was in high school and college, he was writing feature articles for Chicago newspapers, often stories of the Czech and Polish neighborhoods in the suburbs of Cicero and Berwyn where he grew up. He put into words the culture that I, too, had known since childhood. Both of my parents were from large, immigrant Polish families who lived in Cicero. Blei's stories of the Bohemian bakery and making sausage were my family's stories. His stories and his writing had had a powerful impact on me as a young journalism student. And then, at one point, his byline disappeared, and I wondered what had happened to him.

I emailed him immediately, asking if he would meet with me that weekend to tell me more about the class. I had been given a second chance. That weekend I not only met my writing teacher, I was meeting a new friend. We talked about his class and we talked about the old neighborhood, like distant cousins. I also made a reconnaissance trip over to The Clearing to see where I would be immersing myself in nature and writing for an entire week the following June. As I turned left onto the road to campus, my car's tires transitioned from hard asphalt to a cushion of gravel. Stone pillars flanked the entrance and the rustic wooden gate was open wide, welcoming. Thick woodlands immediately enfolded me and with a gentle turn to the right, the world was left behind.

That next June, I had the same experience of coming home. Once safely within the woodlands of The Clearing property, I stopped the car, rolled down the windows, and killed the ignition – just to listen to the forest. The rustle of leaves in the breeze, soft bird calls. I was home. I felt at home. After several minutes, I started the car once again and slowly, reverently, crept through the woods. At the fork, I bore right and entered the sun-drenched Homestead Meadow. After parking the car, I walked past a dormitory of native stone and entered the courtyard, heading for the focal point of the area, the main lodge. In this wondrous space, surrounded by buildings of soft gray stone and weathered log, stone walls, trees, and wildflowers, I again had the feeling of being enfolded.

I found my room in one of the stone buildings. An inviting retreat with warm, hand-crafted maple furniture. On the beds, exquisite hand-sewn quilts, the names of the women who created them meticulously embroidered on the underside corner. This was just the beginning of experiencing the pervasive and gracious hospitality of the staff and others connected to The Clearing. That evening, the bell outside the lodge called everyone into the dining room for our first supper, as it would continue to do all week. We enjoyed all of our meals together in that cozy room, served family style – perhaps thirty of us, seated at three long tables. Many were from Wisconsin, a smattering from Illinois, Michigan and Minnesota, and a few from exotic places like New Mexico.

I was excited and looking forward to the week, yet I admit that I spent the first few days benchmarking myself as a writer against my classmates. Wondering if I was in over my head. I had no reason for all that wondering, and Jens Jensen, the founder of The Clearing, could have told me that. The writers were welcoming. Many very experienced, some not at all, but all collaborative and encouraging. Jens would have told me to expect that, too.

Norb's knowledge about literature and writing, I came to realize, was as deep and wide as the Grand Canyon. In successive years and classes, it didn't matter whether the week's theme was Jewish Literature, The Writer and the Bigger Picture, or Rural Writing. He always had at the ready at least three weeks of readings to share. To be able to soak in all that he wanted to teach was a gift. To listen to the insights and questions of my fellow writers was a gift as well.

Norb was very inclusive and always extended an invitation to his students to sit in as many of the classes as they wanted to. Though I was in the beginner's class, I participated in the advanced class every afternoon because I did not want to miss a single minute of learning. This made it challenging because finishing my homework for each day meant working late into the night. It didn't matter. It didn't seem like work. I was at The Clearing and I was writing. Stretching myself. And for the first time in my life, I was with a group where everyone was a writer. I didn't have to explain to anybody why I was a writer, like I had to back home. All these people already knew, for they had come to that same awareness, that same sense of self. And that common identity drew us together.

All classes at The Clearing culminate in a "show and tell" event on Friday evening. When there are concurrent classes in art, photography, woodworking or similar subjects, students display their work so others can see what the week at The Clearing brought forth. For writing students, the process is far different. Friday night is our "storytelling night." Those who choose can read their work, whether prose or poetry. Each person valiantly

Coming Home to The Clearing

attempts to keep it to a five-minute timeframe. In 2013, our smaller writing group (led by Susan O'Leary) was combined with a class that explored various natural areas of the county. So that Friday night event included a slide show of photographs from their hikes, with music provided by a fellow student, then followed by the writers' reading program. Socializing topped off the evening. Again, Jens would have been proud. This is what his Clearing is all about.

It is not inconsequential that so much learning takes place at The Clearing. I had learned that Jens Jensen designed parks in Chicago as well as the landscaping for estates in its North Shore suburbs; another connection to Chicago for me. His purpose for The Clearing, beyond a hands-on school for his landscape architecture students, was "to clear away all the debris of overstuffed learning, steeped in form and tradition, and get to the source of all wisdom…the soil." To clear out the clamor and clutter in one's mind, in one's heart, in one's life. To open up a space, physical, psychological and spiritual. To live in a vibrant, engaged learning community for a week, in the midst of the great grandeur of the Niagara Escarpment. To reconnect to the land, and to the most natural world. To reconnect with your Self. To provide physical spaces, inside and out, that allow solitary reflection as well as group interaction. Whether it meant staying a night at the Cliff House which clings to the side of the limestone bluff above the bay, or gathering in the dark of the night to tell stories around the crackling bonfire of the council ring, Jensen instinctively created the outdoor environment where this clearing can happen.

You cannot come to this place and be unaffected. Walking to class, footsteps are cushioned by a deep layer of wood shavings. Stopping for a moment to appreciate the spiral design of the maidenhair fern next to the path. Seeing a bed of sleeping poppies at the foot of Mertha's Cabin explode over the course of a week into well over a hundred ruffled orange blooms. Planting oneself in an Adirondack chair near the Schoolhouse, in a meadow created expressly to enjoy the view of far-off Ellison Bluff. Even in inclement weather, lying in bed at night, windows open, it is a delight to listen to the wind buffeting leaves at the tops of tall trees and the steady rhythm of a light rain, and to take in the earthy smell of fresh air in the country. In the Schoolhouse, one can sit in a favorite spot in order to see out the tall, narrow window behind the teacher, the window with the basswood tree just as straight and tall, and the true blue water and sky beyond.

I could not then, and could not now, separate the place, the teacher, and the people. Jensen intentionally crafted this environment, both natural and familial, from his deep values, his passion, and his vision. Norb, as other Clearing instructors, honors Jensen's intent while eliciting the best from students. For many of us who discover our true selves and creative impulses here, Jensen's home has become our home. As he most fervently wanted it to be.

Gloria Zager

Edith Nash, The Clearing, and Norb Blei

Six years passed after my friend Edith Nash died, before I returned to The Clearing; before I could bear to pass the tree we always looked for on the last curve before the field of coreopsis that announced our arrival. We came for Norb Blei's class in writing. Edith and I met there the first time, now thirty years ago. Edith returned every year for the rest of her life with or without me, but that first time we came separately, each for our own reasons and from towns just miles apart.

Edith had written all her life. I imagined her in college sitting on the corner of her professor's desk, her long slim legs crossed and holding her own in whatever the topic of discussion. I had been a prolific writer with the same confidence and exuberance in my youth. In my case, college had somehow wrangled that out of my system. Now years later I was returning with piles of travel journals filled with writing that made even my eyes glaze over. Edith said when we first met that she could not believe that someone from such a little town of only three hundred people had climbed Mount Kilimanjaro. The thing about Edith is that she loved stories and as I found out later, she loved everyone's story. Nothing seemed to ever bore her. Her attentiveness was astounding. So began our friendship, for she listened to my stories.

But first, The Clearing. What a remarkable place, the stone buildings with their tall windows looking out to Lake Michigan, and those legendary home cooked and abundant meals. But the classes were even more memorable. I wanted to write better. My cumbersome prose needed real work. I remember sitting in those first classes listening to Norb read poetry, his voice resonating off those tall school house windows. One of the first lessons was to write Haiku and I thought yes! This is the conciseness, use of image, and succinct word choice that I needed. I remember sitting on the flat rocks along the shore of the lake below the cliffs, writing. That was the year all those tiny green worms fell on my head from the trees that leaned over the cliffs. After that class I thought I would learn to write poetry as a means to improve my prose.

I returned to the Clearing several times with Edith and as the years went by she moved closer to the front of the class and I moved to the back. Norb let me repeat the beginner's class each time and I was content for a long time just listening to writers discuss

Edith Nash, The Clearing, and Norb Blei

writing. But in the end I felt I simply became the person who came with Edith. After that first class though, I wrote poetry exclusively. I was not studied in poetry, had not read it and certainly had not written it before, but after that class with Norb I never left off writing it. To this day I am the writer who seldom writes, but when I do a whole world opens and it is a wonderful thing. As for my travel journals, I never did do much with them, and the raspberry robins of Tasmania or the fierce Katabatic winds flowing off the ice of Antarctica poke through only now and then as single lines in a poem.

After we'd been in that first class together, Edith determined we would meet to write and discuss our writing, our poems. These discussions evolved to include not only writing, but also reading, cooking, eating and traveling. The stories of her life, her intellectual acuity, her openness to new experience, were addicting and, like a fly to honey, I came. Soon after we met, Edith's husband Philleo died, and after a year she began her new life as she called it. Thinking of her influence on my life, I can only tell stories.

For example, she introduced me to a book on Buddhism. A passing fancy for Edith, but it sparked with me and I am a half-Buddhist to this day. Edith said her meditations took place each morning as she chopped the vegetables for whatever she planned to cook that day. Her interests were of an anthropological nature. Everyone's way of life was a study, wonderfully free of most judgment. Always learning, we took classes in Christian history, Jewish history, and at one point she promoted the Seder in the city churches and schools. She was always mixing things together; looking for the kind of acceptance that comes with knowing that one way is not the only way. These dinners were researched meticulously, were magnificent. We hunted all over for matzo flour in our small mid-Wisconsin town, experimented with unleavened breads; the leg of lamb was the best I ever ate. These are Edith's words; many, many dishes were the best she ever ate. Now it is true for me.

Edith returned to The Clearing the summer before she died. She drove herself. She loved it that much, especially Norb. I moved away from her in those last days, convincing myself I was living her life when I wanted to live mine. Coping, I suppose as her illness progressed. I regret having squandered those days I stayed away. Days before she died she told me to go on a trip I had planned, to Bhutan. I always wondered if it was to get me out of the way. She had said she didn't want anyone around her to entice her to stay when it was her time to go. I was high in the Himalayas when I heard she had died. And no spinning of a hundred prayer wheels or the sight of black-necked cranes careening against the sky through the high mountain passes brought her back to me again. She exists for me in the few poems I wrote about her then and without those evenings sitting at her table reading our poems to each other, the writing of poetry disappears into those recesses that are harder and harder to reach, like forgetting the way to a place that one doesn't often visit. And she was not at the Clearing when I returned there one last time.

They say the universe is expanding exponentially, that in a billion years or so the sky will darken as the stars recede. What a wonderful gift, therefore, for me to have lived now, to maintain my couple of stars in an often black sky, to have known Edith Nash, my friend and mentor, and a teacher like Norb Blei, who taught me how to keep all things alive in poetry.

The Year Was 1973...

It was Virginia Woolf who called my attention to the importance of a room of one's own and as I looked around the small private cabin I had been able to reserve, I realized this was the first time in 10 years that I would have that elusive room.

Earlier in the year I had signed up for a writing class at the College of DuPage and through some cosmic magic landed in one of the few classes Norbert Blei was teaching. I immediately felt an advantage with Norbert. I was the only student that had read his piece in the *Chicago Sun Times* about August Derleth, Wisconsin poet and novelist. The piece had stirred me enough to remember it, and here was the writer, in person. I felt I had met a kindred spirit especially when I found we were both currently reading Harry Crew's *Karate Is A Thing of The Spirit*.

That course at COD gave me the nudge I needed to stretch my writing boundaries, and I found myself submitting a piece to the college literary quarterly. One week I came to class and was handed a copy of the latest issue with my poetic prose published. This was heady stuff and I was so elated I shared it with Norbert, and he in turn invited me to The Clearing that summer. The year was 1973 and it was his second year on a path that was to span almost 40 years of teaching at The Clearing, and it was the year that would point me in the direction of a writing life.

I have to admit that I was afraid of what I had signed up for and that fear was to grow stronger before it would lessen. Me, actually a writer, didn't register at the time, and though I didn't take myself too seriously, and thought of this week as a kind of soft adventure, I did have real apprehensions. The doubt revolved around spending a week with other writers and the realization that I was now going to have to participate, and therein was the challenge, even though I was already familiar with Norbert and his nurturing manner.

Those five days of simplicity, from the family style meals, to the casual atmosphere of the classroom setting, and the splendor of the surroundings, were the background music to the angst I experienced. I knew I wanted to write magical realism even before I knew there was such a genre. I thought I was writing ghostly tales of love and redemption and had a story in the works that I wanted to finish that week.

One afternoon while standing on a rock at Europe Bay with the waves from Lake Michigan splashing from what seemed to be all directions while behind me, the quiet setting of woods and green meadows beckoned, I felt a wave of fearlessness wash over me, and I had a defining moment. It was at The Clearing that I really began to be comfortable with the unfamiliar and stepping into the unknown. I learned to trust myself. It was a stepping stone to the courage that would be needed for the journey taking me from my suburban safety to the West Coast and an independent life.

Before the life changing move and with all this new found confidence, I did apply and was hired for a job as a columnist at one of the small Chicago newspapers. Though I didn't leave my day job for many years and I don't have a book of poetry, or a novel, I am and have been for more than a decade a working writer. I write twelve columns a month about love and its many faces, and after all isn't love just another definition of magical realism.

I still have that unfinished story and planned a week at the Clearing in 2013 hopefully to dip back into fiction. Norbert leaving us as he did put a hold on that visit but what I acquired during that week so long ago was more important than the story I was writing. Alongside of my monthly writing assignment I do have a memoir in the works and as busy as he was, Norbert always found time to lend his encouragement and assistance. The words that make the title of my memoir are his, not mine, and now after his death those words resonate on a much deeper level than when he suggested them:
I Thought You'd Always Be There.

Jude Genereaux

Epilogue

"Find me in my books..."

In my experience, there are two kinds of people in Door County: those that love Norbert Blei , and those that didn't know him.

A brilliant, dedicated teacher, a writer that spoke up for keeping safe the treasure that is Door, Norb lived a Wabi-Sabi lifestyle. He had a penchant for finding beauty in the old, the broken, the discarded; wrote about collapsed barns disintegrating into the ground, hung rusted and dented coffee pots in trees as décor and set broken pieces of pottery on the benches near the Coop to admire. He had no yearning for the grandiose or excessive. An amenity to Norb were the birds he tossed sunflower seeds to each morning, or fresh wood chips adorning the path to the Coop.

I've never known anyone who so thoroughly lived his life as he felt it was meant to be. Norb moved through his days driven by instinct, following an energy he felt for a project as it hit him – not always to its conclusion. The ability to prioritize was not one of his characteristics, for if a subsequent bolt of enthusiasm intersected, he was off on a new trail, a new story. The result is that we are finding a treasure trove of unfinished "works in progress" springing from the archives of the Coop and computer files, like morels in the forest; some stories nearly finished, others never to be. The Coop itself will be preserved and moved to a place that will honor the alchemy and spirit that thrived within its cedar-scented walls.

His obsessive curiosity was both Norb's genius and his curse. His interest was immediately engaged by a question on a writing project, an opinion on a new book – a movie, music – or a wisp of an idea that took him directly to a notepad. Our home was stuffed with an estimated 4,000–5,000 books, any one of which he could find at once, going to the exact passage sought. The Coop held the life's work of one man, but would easily fill an entire Literature wing at a small college with books, ideas, research and preparations made over 40 years of Clearing workshops.

Norb often warned that "Artists are difficult to live with – and writers are the worst!", but I tend to believe all who are driven by a passion for their work march to a more insistent beat, myself included. More enduring to recall is the seductive joy and enthusiasm we shared in nearly 19 years of life in sync. The simplicity of long rides through Door, meandering walks through the parks and forests or galleries and pottery shops, and afternoon picnics at Newport were every-day pleasures. An occasional weekend in our favorite city, Milwaukee (sorry Chicago) as well as just being home. Dinner with friends, evenings

"Find me in my books..."

at the AC Tap, Camp David or local programs, were gifts of a synchronicity of spirit shared. But there was so much more we wanted to do ...

I learned much about how to live a life in sync with who one is and what's important, in nearly 20 years of life with Norbert. Too soon we learned the way of death; his peaceful departure changed my perceptions there too, as he quietly slipped away, his last breath on my shoulder. I will miss his presence and the deep resonance of his voice the rest of my life. I found him in his books.

Books by Norbert Blei

Story Collections
The Hour of the Sunshine Now: Short Stories (1978)
The Ghost of Sandburg's Phizzog (1986)

Novels
The Second Novel: Becoming a Writer (1978)
Adventures in an American's Literature (1982)

Non-Fiction
Door Way: The People in the Landscape (1981)
Door Steps (1983)
Door to Door (1985)
Neighborhood (1987)
Meditations on a Small Lake (1987)
Chi-Town (1990)
Chronicles of a Rural Journalist in America (1990)
Winter Book (2002)

Poetry
The Watercolored World (1968)
Paint Me a Picture/Make Me a Poem (1987)

Collections & Anthologies
Wisconsin's Rustic Roads: A Road Less Travelled; Photographs by Bob Rashid, Text By Ben Logan, George Vukelich, Jean Feraca, Norbert Blei and Bill Stokes (1995)
Rooted: Seven Midwest Writers of Place, David Pichaske, Editor; University of Iowa Press (2006)
Spoon River Quarterly 1982, Spoon River Poetry Press, David Pichaske, Editor

Recordings
The Quiet Time, Door County in Winter Readings by Norb Blei/Music by Jim Spector (1997)
Readings from Door Way (1996)

The Internet
Norbert Blei was one of the first to see the power of the internet to engage discussion about writers and writing. His *Poetry Dispatch, Notes from The Underground, Once Upon A Time, North of Kafka, Basho's Road,* and *N.B. Coop News* were blogs/e-newsletters, each with their own editorial focus and voice, that featured short selections of writing by noteworthy poets/writers, as well as brief essays on a wide variety of current topics, literary and otherwise. These blogs/e-newsletters created a loyal, expansive international audience for Norbert's voice.

Patron & Sponsors of *The Professor's Quarters*

Patron
Catherine Hovis

Sponsors
After Hours Press
Anonymous (MS)
Anonymous (NFR)
Sharon Auberle
MaryJo Balistreri
Daniel and Nancy Balz
Christopher Blei
Michael Brecke
Don and Louise Buchholz
Bridget Buff
Charles F. Calkins, The Badger Bibliophile
Jean Casey
Alan Catlin
The Clearing
Daniel Cummings
Alice D'Alessio
Carol Doty
Julie Eger
Richard Finch
Donald Fraker and Maja Jurisic
Barbara Fuhrmann
Jude Genereaux
Susan Hannus
Candace Hennekens
Charlotte Johnston
Ellen Kort
Jean Kozak
Jackie Langetieg
Little Eagle Press
John Maring
Charlie Miller
Susan O'Leary
Sue Peterson
David Pichaske
Elizabeth Pochron
Richard Purinton, Island Bayou Press
Mariann Ritzer
Paul Schroeder
Marie Skrobot
Sled Dog Moon
Thomas Smith, Angst Productions
Tim & Susan Stone
Peter Thelen
Cheryl Welch
Robert Zoschke
Judith Zukerman

www.ingramcontent.com/pod-product-compliance
Lightning Source LLC
Chambersburg PA
CBHW042051290426
44110CB00001B/25